Fourth DIMENSION

Teacher's Guide New Edition

Patricia Mugglestone
with Robert O'Neill

THE FOURTH DIMENSION

Language teaching and learning tends to move within three main dimensions. They are the dimensions of *Intelligibility, Accuracy* and *Fluency*.

This book is concerned not only with these dimensions but with a fourth dimension, as well. What is this Fourth Dimension? The Fourth Dimension is *Expressivity*.

Expressivity means not only the ability to say and write things fairly clearly, accurately and fluently but also to express *what you really want to express* and to give some real *depth* to that expression.

Depth comes from a knowledge of choices in language; choices of vocabulary, choices of structure. *Expressivity* is the ability to use language with an understanding of choices, and of how those choices affect the meaning of what you want to say.

Robert O'Neill

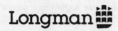

CONTENTS

5 SUCCESS AND FAILURE 24

1 Showing when actions happened

He went into the kitchen, drinking his coffee.
He went into the kitchen and drank his coffee.

When James came back, Joyce had got up.
When James came back, Joyce got up.

2 Definite and cautious assurances

You can depend on us to carry out your instructions.
Your instructions will be carried out.

We should be able We're doing our best	to carry out	your instructions.
We can't see any difficulty in carrying out		

3 I hope so./I hope not.

There's no need to worry.	→	I hope not.
You can depend on us.	→	I hope so.

4 Words and their forms
deliver – delivery, assure – assurance, etc.

5 Vocabulary
Ways of moving: stagger, creep, stroll, etc.

6 Phonology
Stress in compound nouns: tracksuit, sportscar, etc.

6 VOICES FROM NOWHERE 27

1 Expressing assumptions and opinions

He	must is supposed to should	have	killed them here.

2 Having things done

He	redecorated the house.
	had the house redecorated.

3 Reacting to what people say

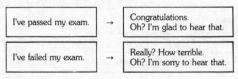

I've passed my exam.	→	Congratulations. Oh? I'm glad to hear that.
I've failed my exam.	→	Really? How terrible. Oh? I'm sorry to hear that.

4 Vocabulary
Belief and disbelief: I doubt/believe/ reject this.

5 Phonology
Stress in verbs and nouns: explain, explanation, etc.

7 SPORT AND VIOLENCE 32

1 Degrees of certainty

Something was thrown.	It must have been an ashtray.
	It might have been an ashtray.

2 despite/although

Despite several bad injuries in his career, Muhammed Ali was never knocked out.

Although he was badly injured several times in his career, Muhammed Ali was never knocked out.

3 Agreeing and disagreeing, with reasons and comments

I hardly ever go to football matches.

↓   ↓

Neither do I. I'm just not interested any more. In fact, I never have been.
Oh, really? I do. I really enjoy a good game. And I like the atmosphere, too.

I think boxing ought to be banned.

↓   ↓

So do I! It's such a violent sport. It's really dangerous.
I don't. I admit it's dangerous sometimes, but it can be a very skilful sport, too.

4 Prepositions
at, on, to, etc.

5 Vocabulary
Sport: boxing, football, tennis, etc.

6 Phonology
Pronunciation of 'ou': count, should, etc.

8 YOUTH AND EXPERIENCE 36

1 Regrets and hopes

I wish	I had children.
	I had had children.

I would like	to have had children.
	to have children.

2 Future in the past

I wish I had known I would like to have known	that I	was going to would	reach this age.

3 Vocabulary
Ways of speaking: shout, murmur, whisper, etc.

4 Phonology
Understanding sentence stress: You know how I feel about you.

9 A HEALTHY LIFE

1 Suggesting that things are easy to do

All you have to do to contact me is phone this number.

2 'be used to'

I am used to	getting a lot of exercise. a lot of exercise.

3 'consider'/'regard'

I	consider you (to be) regard you as	one of my best friends.

4 Cause and effect

Flooding was	caused by due to	the heavy rain.
The reason for the floods was the heavy rain.		

Heavy rain can	lead to result in	flooding.
If there is heavy rain, there may be flooding.		
There was a lot of heavy rain. As a result, there was flooding.		

5 Vocabulary
Different ways of asking: ask, inquire, demand.

6 Phonology
Understanding sentence stress: What are you doing down there?

10 QUESTIONS OF CONSCIENCE

1 Degrees of certainty

	was obviously	
The patient	was apparently seemed to be appeared to be	in great pain.
I had the impression that It seemed to me that		the patient was in great pain.

2 Formal written language and less formal spoken

The man to whom I spoke was a famous surgeon.
The patient was given the injection.

The man I spoke to was a famous surgeon.
I gave the patient the injection.

3 Vocabulary
Describing behaviour: lazy, irresponsible, conscientious, etc.

4 Phonology
Stress in compound adjectives: hard-working, easy-going, etc.

11 THERE'S MORE TO LISTENING THAN HEARING

1 'What' clauses

Listen carefully to what I am going to say.

We let our prejudices distort what a person has to say.

2 'Which' clauses

You speak rather quickly and softly, which makes it difficult to understand you.

3 Gerund

Listening is more difficult than hearing. Learning how to listen requires special training.

4 Words and their forms
efficient–efficiency, respond–response, etc.

5 Phonology
Word stress: Chinese, volunteer, etc.

12 WHAT'S WRONG WITH A LITTLE CRIME?

1 'by', 'by the time' and 'until'

I'll be home by 6 o'clock. I'll be home by the time you finish that.

I'll be home until 6 o'clock.

2 'from' and 'since'

Bonnie met Clyde in 1930. From that time until their deaths, they were partners.

W.D. Jones was pardoned after spending several years in prison. Since then, nothing has been heard of him.

3 'if' and 'in case'

Take this shotgun if you need it.

Take this shotgun in case you need it.

4 'if' and 'unless'

I never shoot people if they try to stop me.

I never shoot people unless they try to stop me.

5 Vocabulary
Criminals and their crimes: murderer–murder, thief–theft, etc.

6 Phonology
Word stress: psychiatrist, carpenter, politician, etc.

13 THE UNCLE I HARDLY KNEW 55

1 'feel like' and 'feel as if'

I feel like swimming.

I feel as if I were swimming.

2 Forbidding and saying that things are not necessary or advisable

You don't	need have	to do that.

You mustn't It is forbidden to You shouldn't	do that.

3 Prepositions
at, on, to, etc.

4 Vocabulary
a) Phrasal verbs: let (someone) down, let out, let on, etc.
b) Feelings and perceptions about the world around us: sensation, impression, illusion, delusion.

5 Phonology
Word stress: Photography, Photographer, Photographic, etc.

14 THE PRICE OF AN EDUCATION 59

1 Repeated actions in the past

My father was always saying education was a waste of time.

My mother kept telling him I was university material.

My father would turn the radio up full volume.

2 Encouraging/discouraging someone and reporting this

'Why don't you learn shorthand? It would be useful.'

↓

He encouraged her to learn shorthand.

'Don't start smoking. It's terrible for your health.' 'I don't see any point in your learning shorthand.'

↓

He discouraged her from smoking/ learning shorthand.

3 Gerund or infinitive?

What's the use of	speaking French?

There's no need She helped me She had a chance	to speak French.

She	prevented me from got used to looked forward to had a chance of was afraid of had great difficulty in got better at	speaking French.

4 Vocabulary
School, study and education: education, training, instruction, etc.

5 Phonology
Saying the same thing with two different meanings: What are you learning shorthand for?

15 NIGHT AND DAY 63

1 Emphasizing what you are saying

I *do* remember the birds. They *did* sing beautifully.

He's impolite but he *is* a good cook. I knew you *were* lazy but I *had* hoped you would pass *one* of your exams.

2 Explaining and describing

It	is can be	used to clean things with.

It	is made of wood.
	consists of three parts.
	looks something like a metal box.

3 Words and their forms
science–scientific, excite–excitement, etc.

4 Vocabulary
Sounds of animals: purr, roar, quack, etc.
Characteristics of animals: cunning fox, busy bee, etc.

5 Phonology
Emphasising what you are saying: Birds are often dirty but they do sing beautifully.

Tapescripts of listening dialogues 68

INTRODUCTION

Who is *Fourth Dimension* **for?**

1 This book can be used in adult courses and by teenage learners at upper secondary level. It is designed for what is often called the upper intermediate level, which is typically the level of the fourth book in most courses. It can be used after Third Dimension or following the third book of many textbook series in use all over the world.

2 Learners at this level have often reached a kind of 'plateau'. They have covered all or a great deal of the 'core language' in a communicative syllabus but often lack confidence in using it. They often fail to appreciate or fully grasp some rather basic distinctions in English, such as 'I am here for three weeks' and 'I've been here for three weeks' or 'You mustn't do that' and 'You don't need to do that'. They may 'know' such things at a conscious level and if they are given time to reflect on them, but they still do not always use them fluently or understand their full meaning.

3 This book takes students up to a level equivalent to that of the Cambridge First Certificate examination but it does not provide specific examination practice.

How long does it take?

It is always difficult to estimate the exact number of contact hours necessary for any coursebook. The exact number is *always* dependent on a number of factors usually beyond the control of the teacher or the coursewriters.

However, in normal circumstances (if circumstances are ever 'normal') *Fourth Dimension* will need *at least* 70 contact hours and can easily generate a full 100 contact hours. Teaching and learning do not stop with the book, nor should they be completely restricted to it (unless there is simply no time to go beyond it). Each unit can be developed and extended in a great variety of ways.

The number of contact hours can also be affected by what you decide to do with the material in the book. You can, for example,

a) use the Language study sections for work in class, or simply assign them as homework;

b) divide the class at times into separate groups and get them to work on different tasks within the unit;

c) increase or decrease the discussion time devoted to various questions and topics in the book;

d) choose to omit certain useful but *optional* activities within each unit.

This (d) applies particularly to all the unseen listening activities for which there is no written text in the unit itself. As useful as listening is, experience in various parts of the world, including highly developed countries such as Japan and Germany, has convinced the authors that conditions and equipment are too variable, too unreliable in many places, for them to insist that such listening activities should always take place or be prescriptive about how they are done.

What does the course consist of?

The course has four components

Coursebook (15 units)
Teacher's Guide (full notes on each unit, including answer key where necessary and tapescripts for all unseen listening)
Study Book (provides language practice for out-of-class study, reinforces language and skills practised in coursebook, answer key for independent checking and correction)
Cassette (recordings of all dialogues and unseen listening tasks)

Although each unit varies in some way or other, there is always some kind of short text, a dialogue, usually an unseen listening activity, and always a *Language study* section which covers both grammatical/functional work and vocabulary as well. There is also work on intonation and stress in all units.

Each unit ends with a STUDY SECTION. This is different in design and purpose from *Language study*. The STUDY SECTION sums up the main language points in each unit. It gives a writing task and a self-check exercise. These writing tasks develop progressively from unit to unit. Although this section is intended to be used at home, it can also be used in class in a variety of ways if time permits.

The Study Book provides further language practice for home and private study. It reinforces and extends the language and skills practised in the Coursebook. At the same time, it aims to develop the student's confidence in his/her own learning abilities and to lead to more independent learning strategies. The types of exercise found in the Study Book are grammar, vocabulary, dictionary work, reading, conversation management, puzzles and exercises which focus on language learning. An answer key ensures that students can work independently and check their own work. However, each unit in the Study Book ends with a freer and more personal exercise, 'What about you?', which the teacher is invited to look at, not only to check the language but to get to know individual students better. Exercises such as 'What about you?', conversation management and language learning are also suitable for students to work on and develop in small 'study groups' out-of-class: the exercises provide them with a framework for making conversations, talking about themselves and their own language learning experiences. The tests which occur after units 5, 10 and 15 can be used as self-checking progress tests or as class tests.

What is the basic methodology ?

The course is based on the concept that it is not enough simply 'to understand' or that comprehension, by itself, can lead to any real fluency in language use. In order even to understand a language in a more than superficial way, you have to use it. The materials in each unit promote and encourage a variety of uses.

We assume also that some conscious learning, including conscious study of grammar rules, can be useful and is indeed in many cases even essential. It is true that some – perhaps most – of the most important 'rules' we form about language use are unconscious, and never fully available to conscious reflection or explanation. However, such conscious rules can help guide and inform our creative, largely unconscious and spontaneous use of language. Without some conscious 'mental picture' of a language or the main parts of its system, it is difficult for many learners to continue learning independently. And the purpose of all books and all teaching, particularly at this level, must be to develop the learner's powers of independent learning. This,

too, is part of the 'Fourth Dimension' of learning, from which this book takes its title.

This is why there is, in each unit, a variety of opportunities for learners to use language spontaneously, to express opinions and feelings, and even to talk about subjective associations which do not depend directly on the text itself. There are also many different kinds of opportunity to develop their cognitive awareness of how the language works, to extend their range of choice in structure and vocabulary, to see how the structure of a sentence, far from being 'just grammar' is a basic part of the meaning of that sentence.

A few suggestions on using the material

It is not and cannot be the purpose of this introduction or any part of this Teacher's Guide to dictate how material should be used. Any teaching material that is any good is capable of being used in all sorts of ways which the authors could never have foreseen. Teaching conditions, even within one school, vary too much for simple recipes to be useful.

However, there are a few things that are true for wherever this book is likely to be used. Some of them are obvious. But perhaps it is the most obvious that needs saying, since it is often the most obvious that we all forget to do at times.

1 Don't use the reading texts only for reading. Reading, like all comprehension, is not a passive activity. Get the class to explore the text at different levels. See the detailed teaching notes for each unit for various suggestions about how to do this.

2 Give the class time to do the discussion and role play activity. This again may seem obvious. But in practice it is often hard for teachers to get out of the way when it is necessary. As teachers, we tend to be threatened by silence. We tend to rush activities along or get worried if they don't 'take off' immediately.

3 If possible, break up the Language study with other activities. Because things are printed in a certain order on the page does not mean you have to do them in that order. The printed order of items on a page is often a matter of visual convenience. Thus, grammar items are

put together in one section on a page. But in teaching, it may be better to change that order. For example, language points can often be dealt with between the general comprehension phase of a reading text and the more detailed comprehension.

4 Try to create an atmosphere of relaxed but alert concentration in the class.

A state of relaxed rather than anxious concentration favours language learning and assimilation. Teachers have to be aware not only of their methods but of themselves as physical beings. Facial expression, body movement and pace of speech are crucial teaching tools. If the teacher looks threatening or censorious, students will become defensive and will not learn as well as they would in an atmosphere of mutual trust and co-operation. This is obvious. But it is not always acted upon.

5 Use recorded listening material only if your equipment (cassette player, etc.) is adequate.

All the unseen listening material (where there is no script for students to read) is *optional.* But it is all very useful material. However, it is better not to use it at all rather than use it on a machine that is too small, has a bad speaker or is in other ways inadequate.

Remember also that, if necessary, you can read the texts aloud yourself. This is often preferable in very large classes or in noisy surroundings - let's say, a classroom near a main road in a busy town with the windows open.

6 Encourage students to react to and talk about the visuals in the book and the recordings. These provide opportunities for students to express their own responses to and ideas about characters and settings depicted in pictures and sound.

7 Take a sympathetic attitude towards students' mistakes. Don't expect students to be accurate all the time, even with very basic structures. Accuracy, even with basic things, comes slowly. It is usually preceded by fluency. When correcting, try to get students to correct their own mistakes. Sometimes, don't correct at all, especially when correcting would break the flow of what a student is trying to say or would make that student too conscious of form to concentrate on meaning. The best time to go for accuracy is in written work and in the *Language study* sections. The rest of the time, it is often best to correct only if and when a mistake seriously interferes with meaning. Good examples are when even advanced learners sometimes say 'she' instead of 'they' or 'he' or confuse some of the forms you can find in the *Language study* section under 'What's the difference in meaning?'

Reference Books

Where it is considered appropriate, or helpful, references are given in the Teaching Notes to *A Communicative Grammar of English* (Fifteenth Impression 1988), by Geoffrey Leech and Jan Svartvik, published by Longman.

We also recommend that students use a good monolingual dictionary, such as the *Longman Dictionary of Contemporary English* (New Edition 1987) or the *Longman Active Study Dictionary of English* (Eighth Impression 1987).

1 ALONE IN THE CROWD

Overview of the Unit

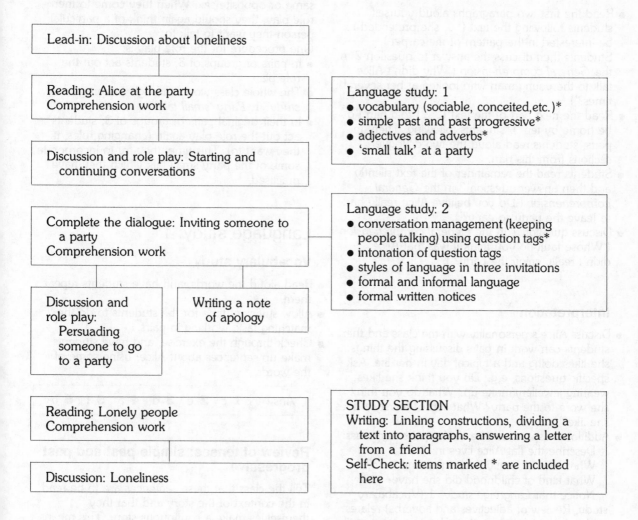

Lead-in: Discussion about loneliness

Reading: Alice at the party
Comprehension work

Discussion and role play: Starting and
continuing conversations

Complete the dialogue: Inviting someone to
a party
Comprehension work

Discussion and
role play:
Persuading
someone to go
to a party

Writing a note
of apology

Reading: Lonely people
Comprehension work

Discussion: Loneliness

Language study: 1
● vocabulary (sociable, conceited,etc.)*
● simple past and past progressive*
● adjectives and adverbs*
● 'small talk' at a party

Language study: 2
● conversation management (keeping
people talking) using question tags*
● intonation of question tags
● styles of language in three invitations
● formal and informal language
● formal written notices

STUDY SECTION
Writing: Linking constructions, dividing a
text into paragraphs, answering a letter
from a friend
Self-Check: items marked * are included
here

Lead-in

● Read out the title of the unit (*Alone In The
Crowd*) and ask students, 'What does it mean?
Have you ever had the feeling of being alone in
a large group of people? Is being alone the same
as being lonely?'
Encourage students to discuss and speculate
about the photograph.
One procedure is:
● Read all the questions aloud.
● Ask students to think about questions 1-4 for a
few minutes, and talk to their neighbour about

them if they want to. Then, have a class
discussion.
● In groups of 3 or 4, students can then discuss
questions 5-7.
● Finally, students may like to ask you if you
have ever felt lonely and what you did about it.
You may notice that students are having some
problems with basic question forms during this
activity. Avoid too much correction during the
questioning – the emphasis here is on building
confidence in communicating. However, make a
mental note of their problems for later remedial
work.

Reading/General comprehension

- Read the first two paragraphs aloud yourself, students following the text ('... she pretended to be interested in the pattern of the carpet'). Students then discuss the answer to question 2 in the *General comprehension* ('Why didn't Alice talk to the young man who looked at her several times?').
- Read the next part of the text ('... I told him I'd be home by ten.'), students following. Then, in pairs, students read aloud the two dialogue sections from this part.
- Students read the remainder of the text silently and then answer question 3 in the *General comprehension* ('Do you believe Alice really had to leave the party so early?').
- Discuss question 1 in the *General comprehension* ('Whose fault do you think it was that Alice didn't really enjoy the party?').

Interpretation

- Discuss Alice's personality with the class and then students can work in pairs discussing the things she likes doing and a typical day in her life. Ask specific questions, e.g. 'Do you think she likes wearing jewellery/make-up? What do you think she wore to the party? What sort of hairstyle does she like?'
- Additional aspects can be set for pairs to discuss:
  Describe the flat Alice lives in.
  What kind of family does she come from?
  What kind of childhood did she have?
  Notice that *Language study*: 1 (Vocabulary study, Review of adjectives and adverbs) relates to this *Interpretation* section. Weaker classes will find it helpful to do these *Language study* exercises before the *Interpretation*.

Focus on details

Students work in pairs, referring back to the text to support their answers.

Discussion and role play

During the discussion, encourage students to consider what they would say to different types of

people, e.g. older or younger than themselves, same or opposite sex. When they come to the role play, they should again think of a particular person they want to talk to.
One procedure for the role play is:
- In pairs or groups of 3, students act out the role play.
- The whole class works through *Language study*: 1, *Party 'small talk'*.
- In their original pairs or groups of 3, students act out the role play again (changing roles, if they want to). This time, they try to incorporate some of the party small talk which they have practised.

Language study: 1

Vocabulary study

- Read aloud the words, and have students repeat them.
- Allow sufficient time for the students to do the matching task, working in pairs.
- Check through the exercise, and have students make up sentences about Alice, using some of the words.

> *Answers*: **1** c **2** e **3** d **4** a **5** f **6** b

Review of tenses: simple past and past progressive

Tell the class that these sentences are to be read in the context of the story and that they themselves make a continuous story. This means that sentence 6 is likely to be 'He looked at her and smiled but she looked away' and sentence 7 is likely to be 'Margaret wondered whether Alice was having fun.'
Teacher's reference: *A Communicative Grammar of English* **122–127** (the progressive aspect).

> *Answers*: **1** got, was standing **2** looked, was preparing **3** came, was sitting **4** came, continued **5** noticed, was talking **6** looked, smiled, looked **7** wondered, was having **8** left, was still going on

Review of adjectives and adverbs

This exercise could be set as homework, after reading through the example sentences.
Teacher's reference: *A Communicative Grammar of English* **463** relates to item 6 (quiet/quietly) in the exercise.

> *Answers*: **1** doubtful **2** doubtfully
> **3** happily **4** happy **5** quiet **6** quiet/
> quietly **7** nervously **8** nervously
> Check that students have spelt doubtfully
> (2) and happily (3) correctly.

Party 'small talk'

- Tell the class that these sentences do not form a continuous story, but are fragments of conversations overheard at a party.
- Students close their books. You read out the prompts in the top column, and students respond to each one spontaneously.
- Students open their books and do the exercise in pairs.
- Check the exercise with the whole class and compare their initial spontaneous responses with reposes a) – h).

> *Answers*: **1** c **2** f **3** d **4** a **5** h **6** g
> **7** b **8** e

- Use the artwork on these pages to give further practice. Ask students to look at the characters and guess what they do for a living – who could be an artist/a writer/a businessman/a journalist/a politician/a private detective? Ask them to imagine what they are talking about – who is saying 'Have you heard the latest scandal. . ?'/'A bit chilly this evening, isn't it?'/'Would you like to come round to my place afterwards for some coffee'/'Don't look now, but there's an extremely strange-looking person over there.'?

Dialogue

Complete the dialogue/Questions

- Students work individually, reading through the dialogue and trying to fill in the gaps. Then, in pairs, they discuss and compare their answers.

- Go through the dialogue with the whole class, writing the suggested answers on the board.
- Look at question 4 with the whole class and fill in the given words in the dialogue. Compare these answers with the students' suggestions on the board.
- Go through questions 1–3 with the class. After answering the questions, students can work in pairs, creating dialogues in which 'Margaret invited Alice to a party and Alice was eager to come' (b) or 'Even though Margaret insisted that she should come, Alice refused' (d). This second situation will provide useful preparation for the role play which follows.
Notice that it is appropriate to include *Language study: 2*, (conversational question tags) here. Draw students' attention to the way question tags are used in the dialogue, and then go on to the *Language study: 2* sections. This will also prepare students for the later *Discussion and role play* section.

> *Answers*: **1** c. If some of the class thought the correct answer was 'a', help them to work out why it is not, by asking:
> (i) I'm having a party and I want you to come. What do I say to you? (Can you/ Would you like to come?)
> (ii) If I say to you, 'Let's go to the party', whose party is it – mine or someone else's? (Someone else's.)
> **4** The missing words in the dialogue are
> **1** i **2** h **3** b **4** f **5** d **6** g **7** j **8** a **9** e
> **10** c.

- Play the taped dialogue once for students to hear the complete dialogue. Ask them if Margaret and Alice sound as they imagined they would, or not – if not, how had they imagined they would sound? Then, replay the tape, this time pausing to ask students what Alice is thinking (which may not be the same as she is saying). For example, pause after: Well, I'd like to very much/I've got some work to do/Well, all right, then. It's very nice of you to invite me.

Discussion and role play

- Elicit some examples of the language used when persuading someone to do something. Tell the class 'You think I need more exercise and so you want to persuade me to come along with you to a Keep Fit course. What do you say to me?' Write their suggestions on the board, e.g. You really should .../Why don't you ...?

- Look at the situation in the book. Students work in pairs, thinking of the actual words they would use. (They can make notes if they want to.)
- Students act out their role plays, without referring to their notes.

Writing

If students are not used to writing such short letters, do this as a class exercise and write the note on the board. Check that students know where to write the address and date and how to begin and end the note of apology. This will be useful preparation for the written work in the STUDY SECTION of this unit.

Example answer

(Address)
(Date)
Dear A,

     I've just remembered that I'll be away on Saturday and so won't be able to come to your party after all. I really am sorry about this. Hope you have a very good party. See you soon.

Yours,

B

Language study: 2

When are questions really questions?

- Read the introductory explanation to the class.
- Tell students to look at question 1 (Nice day today, isn't it?) and imagine that they are in a train or in a café and making conversation with the person next to them. Have two or three students say it aloud. Comment on their intonation.
- Go through the examples, saying them yourself and getting individual students to repeat them after you.
- Ask the class what the other person would reply,

e.g. 'Nice day today, isn't it?' – 'Yes, it is.'
- Students now work in pairs, going through all the sentences, with the second person responding each time.
Teacher's reference: *A Communicative Grammar of English* **250**

Make conversation!

Students work in pairs, student **A** asking the question with a question tag, and student **B** responding. Then students change roles.

How sure are you of the answer?

- The intonation of the question tags in the dialogue is:
1 rising   2 falling   3 falling   4 falling
The falling intonation indicates that the speaker is almost sure of the answer whereas the rising intonation indicates that the speaker is less sure. Notice that the answer to question 4 is not the one which Margaret expects.
- Students work in pairs. Student A chooses whether to use a rising or falling intonation and Student B says whether the voice goes up or down.

Three styles of language

When students have identified the styles, ask them what it is about 1 which suggests speaking informally, compared with speaking formally in 2. Students can then suggest how they would reply to each invitation, both accepting it and declining it.

Change the form

Students work in groups of 3 or 4, writing down their answers. Allow them sufficient time to think about and discuss the examples.

Answers: the following are appropriate ways of being formal and polite.
1 Would you like
2, 4, 5, 8 Would you mind—ing/Could you/Do you think you could
3 I hope you'll let me
6 (Excuse me, but) you're not allowed
7 (Excuse me, but) could you

12

Writing

This could be given as homework. If students are living in an English-speaking environment, they can make a note of other notices they see in shops, streets, on buses, etc. The class can then discuss these notices in a future lesson.

> *Example answers*: **5** Turn off lights before leaving. **6** No parking. **7** Dogs not allowed.

Reading

True or false?

- Before reading the text, ask students to look at the true/false statements, and predict the answers, using their own experience and knowledge.
- Students now read the text individually (silently) and answer the true/false questions from the text.
- Discuss with the class any differences between their predicted answers and the answers based on the text.

> *Answers*: **1** false **2** true **3** false

Vocabulary

Students do this in pairs.

> *Answers*: **1** c **2** a **3** a **4** b

Discussion and interpretation

Students discuss the questions in groups of 3 or 4. A spokesperson from each group can then report back the answers to questions 1 and 2, and the class can see if all the groups agree about the kinds of people most likely to feel lonely.

STUDY SECTION

Writing skills

- Introduce the exercise in class. Ask students to read the text quickly, trying to answer these two questions: 'What else do we find out about Margaret's party? What impression do you get of Margaret's sister?'
- Discuss the answers together.
  If your students are not used to writing letters, do part 3 in class, building up the paragraphs on the board to give them a model. They can then follow this model and write their own paragraphs at home.

> *Answers*: **1** **1** f **2** d **3** e **4** i
> **5** c **6** b **7** g **8** h **9** a
> **2** Most likely divisions are paragraph 2 starting 'By the time our first guests arrived …' and paragraph 3 starting 'I wonder what you've …'

Language summary

It is helpful to draw students' attention to the Language summary when you have finished a unit in class. Read through the summary together, getting students to create new examples of their own to check that they have understood and can use these forms. The summary should then provide a helpful learning aid for home study and revision.

Self-Check

Explain to the class that this is a self-checking exercise, to be done at home and checked by looking at the answer key. Students should make a note of any problems they have and ask you in the next lesson.

> *Answers*: **1** enjoyable **2** wasn't it?
> **3** passed **4** quickly **5** shouldn't we
> **6** had **7** was driving **8** saw **9** drove
> **10** slowly **11** realized **12** was burning
> **13** fiercely **14** were trying **15** stopped
> **16** came **17** dangerous **18** put
> **19** wasn't it?

2   QUESTIONS OF HONESTY

Overview of the unit

Lead-in: Pair/group discussion saying what you would do in three given situations

Reading: A case of shop-lifting
Comprehension work and speculating about what you would/might have done in the same situation*

Language study: 1
● vocabulary (glimpse, peer at, etc.)*
● describing what you saw (complete and incomplete actions)*: re-tell a story, write the middle of a story, tell someone about something unusual which you saw or heard

Writing the final paragraph of the story

Listening: Two people say what they would have done in this situation

Discussion: 'White lies'
What would you say in three given situations?

Dialogue: Making excuses for being late
Read the dialogue
Comprehension work
Listen to the dialogue

Language study: 2
● intonation, stress and the use of question tags when being sarcastic

STUDY SECTION
Writing: Completing a letter to a friend (giving reasons, describing an event, describing future plans)
Prepositions of place and movement
Self-Check: items marked * are included here

Lead-in

● Read situation 1 and ask students what they would do. If necessary, put on the board:
I might .../I think I'd .../I probably would ...
Then, get students to tell you what they would *say* in this situation. The best way to do this is for

you to take the role of the cashier yourself first.

T: *(pretending to count out money)* Three pounds fifty. Four pounds. Five. Ten.

Now wait and see what the class tells you.

T: (*motioning for response*) What do you say? Remember. You've just given me £5.

• Students discuss the illustration for situation 2, speculating about the woman. Encourage them to talk about her background (Has she got any family? Is she rich or poor?), her personal history (How old is she? What sort of life has she had? What sort of work did she do? Is she married? Has she got any hobbies or interests?), her home (Does she live in her own house or rent a room somewhere? What is it like? What sort of street does she live in? What sort of neighbours has she got?)

• Students can work in small groups, discussing what they would do and say in situations 2 and 3. Finally, some of the groups can act out the situations for the rest of the class.

Reading/ Questions

Use the five questions as pre-questions to direct students' reading. Ask them to read the first paragraph and find the answer to question 1. Check this answer, then get students to read to the end of the story and answer the remaining questions. *Language study: 1, Vocabulary study* could be done at this stage in order to draw students' attention to these items in the reading text.

Discussion and interpretation

Students discuss these questions in groups of 4, then report back to the whole class. If some of the groups have different suggestions for the ending of the story, get them to act out the alternative endings, taking the parts of Jennifer, Mr Patel and the two boys. This oral work is good preparation for the writing task.

Writing

• Remind students of useful expressions to link events in a story:
then, as soon as, after, before, immediately, by the time, etc.

• Students write the paragraph working in pairs.

Then, in groups of 4, the pairs exchange their paragraphs, read and comment on them.

Listening

First, tell the students to listen and find out what each speaker would do. Play the cassette, and discuss the answers. Then go on to the questions in the book, replaying the cassette as many times as necessary.

> *Answers:* **1** Speaker **B** **2** hesitates less, sounds more certain – 'it's quite clear what I should have done'
> **3** 'it would have depended on various things', 'or something like that', 'so I can't really say' **4** 'At least ... at least, that's what I ought to have done!'

Language study: 1

Vocabulary study

After doing the exercise, elicit other verbs connected with *seeing* which students know (*wink, blink, squint, gaze, peep, scan*). Each student can select one verb to mime, annnd the rest of the class guess what it is.

> *Answers:* **1a** stare **b** peer **c** catch a glimpse of **d** glance **2a** stare
> **b** glance **c** catch a glimpse of **d** peer

What's the difference in meaning?
• Students work in groups of 3 or 4, reading and discussing the example sentences. They will probably work out the difference in meaning for themselves.
• With the whole class, read the *Comment* section, and have students make up sentences using *watch, see, hear* and *listen to.*

Tell the story

After doing the 10 sentences in the exercise, ask students to close their books. Give them the first sentence 'Late in the night someone banged on

15

your door' and then ask individuals to continue the narrative. It doesn't matter if they change the original sequence of events. The main aim is to compose a well-connected 'chain story'.

Write the story

This could be given for homework or done individually in class. Pairs of students can then exchange stories and read and comment on each other's work.

Think about it

Allow students sufficient time to think out what they are going to say so that they can aim for both accuracy and fluency when telling their anecdotes. The activity can be done in small groups. Each group then selects one of its anecdotes to tell the rest of the class.

Discussion

This discussion provides a lead-in to the following Dialogue.

What would you say?

After the pair discussions of the three situations in the book, ask students to suggest other situations in which 'white lies' are often told. Be prepared to give some examples of your own (a friend asks you if you like his/her new clothes/hairstyle/flat. You don't, but you know he/she does. What do you say?)

Dialogue

Interpretation/Listening

- Follow the procedure outlined in the Coursebook.
- Students read the dialogue silently. Allow them sufficient time to read it through at least twice.
- In pairs, students discuss the answers to the Interpretation questions, then discuss the answers with the whole class. Encourage students to

speculate about the people and the situation, defending their own points of view. Accept their ideas and do not tell them what the 'correct' answers are at this stage.
- Before playing the cassette, ask two students to read the dialogue aloud. They can then compare their version with that on the cassette. Discuss the Listening questions with the whole class. Play the cassette again, pausing it appropriately, when answering question 3. This will prepare students for the intonation work in *Language study: 2*.

Language study: 2

Understanding intonation

Notice that this relates directly to speaker **B**'s intonation in the previous dialogue, and so should be done immediately after the dialogue work. The main aim is that students should recognize when someone is being sarcastic. Not all of them will want to sound sarcastic themselves. The practice can be extended by asking students, in their pairs or threes, to make up short (4–line) dialogues containing one of the example sentences. The groups then read out their dialogues, and the rest of the class decide if they sound sarcastic, or not.

Saying things sarcastically

Give students sufficient time to work out the question tags before practising the sarcastic intonation.

STUDY SECTION

Writing skills

Explain that Jennifer is writing to a friend and ask the class to read through the letter quickly and find out something about this friend (he is visiting Jennifer next weekend, he is a keen photographer). Read the letter aloud, eliciting suggestions for the missing parts 1–3. If necessary, these could be written on the board. Students can then complete the letter for homework, together with the postscript, which revises prepositions from the reading text.

Students can be referred to Study Notes on prepositions in the *Longman Active Study Dictionary*, pages 474–5.

Answers: **4** e **5** d **6** a **7** h **8** b
9 c **10** g **11** f

Self-Check

Answers: **1** watching **2** doing
3 witnessed **4** playing **5** glanced
6 put **7** take **8** would **9** stare
10 should **11** would

When the class has done the Self-Check exercise, it can be used to give further oral practice, using the same technique as in *Tell the story* earlier in the unit. Students close their books and then re-tell the story, using their imagination and adding information if they want to.

3 DANGEROUS ILLUSIONS

Overview of the unit

Lead-in: dialogue (telling people how much they mean to you) – 'love', 'be fond of', 'care for', 'mean a lot to'*

Reading: Two texts: 'Julia' and 'Dennis'
Comprehension work

Listening: Full interview with Dennis

Language study: 1
● modals (is going to/will; may/might; ought to/should)*
● words and their forms, including prepositions which follow (argue with someone/argument)*

Find the dialogue: Dennis accuses his girlfriend, Cynthia, of lying to him
Comprehension work

Listening: Full dialogue between Dennis and Cynthia

Language study: 2
● 'Have you seen him?' and 'Have you been seeing him?'*
● 'I was going to tell you' and 'I am going to tell you'*
● word stress (influence; influential)

Reading: Romantic love versus rational love
Comprehension work

Discussion: What qualities do you look for when you fall in love?

STUDY SECTION
Writing: Identifying expressions found in formal written English. Writing a confidential assessment of someone's strengths and weaknesses.
Self-Check: items marked * are included here

Dialogue/Questions

Students read the dialogue silently and discuss question 1 – who do you think **A** and **B** are? Then, play the dialogue on cassette and see if students have any more comments on **A** and **B** before discussing the rest of the questions.

Reading and comprehension work

Put on the board: *age? job? problem?* Half the class then reads the text about Julia while the other half reads about Dennis.

Afterwards, students tell each other about Julia and Dennis, answering the questions on the board and adding any other information they can remember. Each text can then be read aloud by you or the students and the more intensive comprehension work done. Finally, listen to the interview with Dennis and ask students to note down the extra things that Dennis says. Ask students what impressions they have of Dennis now that they have heard the interview, and also what they think of the interviewer.

Answers: (**Explain the words**) **1** *it* – I meet an attractive, intelligent man ... I can't even stand the sight of him **2** *It* – (one of the) small, irritating things **3** *feel the way I do* – feel I don't really love him after all **4** *him* – the attractive, intelligent man **5** *it* – (that I will) ever meet a man I can really love **6** *that* – have at least one child before I get much older.

Answers: (**Listening**): Extra information – he feels it is important not to drift into a relationship because he is lonely. Sometimes he is lonely, but he knows he can live alone and this would be better than marrying someone who isn't really what he wants.

Language study: 1

Review of basic modals

Teacher's reference: *A Communicative Grammar of English* **130** (be going to), **293–5** (may, might), **300–1** (will), **343** (should, ought to), **501** (modals). Students can be referred to the Study Notes on modal verbs in the *Active Study Dictionary* (pages 386–7).

Using modals

Answers: **1** ought to/should **2** may/might **3** will/is going to **4** should/ought to **5** may/might **6** will/am going to

After doing the exercise, students close their books. Ask them to reply in a similar way to your questions.
Ask questions such as, 'Are you going to bed early tonight?' 'Are you going to do your homework this week?' 'Do you think it'll be hot tomorrow?' Include questions about topical events and your students' interests and hobbies.

What about you?

Students work in groups of 3 or 4. Encourage them to correct themselves and each other if mistakes are made. Here, the emphasis is on accuracy as well as fluency.

Word forms

Work through the examples with the whole class. Then, either set the exercise for homework, or have students do it in pairs in class. If students have reliable monolingual dictionaries, you could allow them to use these if they wish. This will provide useful training in dictionary reference skills.

Answers: **1** attractive **2** attracted to/by **3** irritating **4** irritated by **5** marry **6** marriage **7** annoyed with **8** annoying **9** annoy **10** argument **11** arguing with **12** suggestion **13** suggested to **14** relationship **15** agree with **16** got married to

Dialogue

Find the dialogue

- Read the introduction to the class, and ask how they think Dennis would react in this situation. 'Would he be very jealous? Would he think there was a good reason why Cynthia was having a meal with an old boyfriend? Do the students think there is anything wrong in this?'
- Read sentences 1–7 aloud to the class, pausing after each one to allow students time to think and predict what might be said afterwards.
- Now, ask students to look at responses a) – g), as you read aloud Dennis's first sentence. Ask students to find Cynthia's reply (d, or possibly c). Do the same with Dennis's second utterance, then let students complete the activity in pairs.
- When the pairs have finished, they can read the dialogue aloud, still working in pairs.

Answers: **1** d **2** c **3** g **4** a **5** f **6** b **7** e

Explain the words

> *Answers:* **1** is over **2** why didn't you tell me **3** lied to me **4** did it end more than a year ago **5** if it is true that he phoned you and said he had some business to discuss with you **6** I'm not jealous

Listening

> *Answers:* **1** The business was a legal matter. Steve wondered if Dennis would be willing to help him.
> **2** When Cynthia said she was going to see her mother, she had intended to see her, but Steve phoned later.

Ask students to give their impressions of Dennis and Cynthia after they have listened to the cassette (appearance, personality).

Language study: 2

Discuss the difference

Teacher's reference: *A Communicative Grammar of English* **116** (present perfect and continuous). Students work in pairs, discussing the sentences. Then, check the answers with the whole class.

Compare the meaning/Questions

Do these two sections together, so that the Questions guide the students' discussion of the pairs of sentences. This could be given for homework, or done in small groups.

> *Answers:* **1** 5a/b **2** 4b **3** 4a **4** 1a
> **5** 1b **6** 2b **7** 3a **8** 6a

What is the difference in meaning?

Teacher's reference: *A Communicative Grammar of English* **130** (am going to), **136** (was going to)

> *Answers:* **1** I was going to, but (I forgot).
> **2** I was going to do it, but ... **3** Just as I was going to phone, my neighbour called.
> **4** I'm going to tomorrow. **5** I was going to invite you to a party.

Stress in nouns adjectives

Students can look up the words in their dictionaries to check the stress in the adjective forms if they are uncertain. The stress changes in 1 2 3 8.

Reading and discussion/General comprehension

As a lead-in activity, write on the board: *rational, romantic*. First, students work by themselves, writing down associations that come to mind for each word. Then, in groups of 3 or 4, they compare and discuss their associations. Finally, as a class, discuss what these words might mean when used with 'love'. Students then go on to read the text, and see if their ideas are the same as Charles Zastrow's.

Discussion

Some classes may enjoy doing this as a 'class questionnaire', in the following way:

- Have a short 'brain-storming' session. Students suggest all the qualities they can think of and these are written on the board.
- One group of students then makes the questionnaire. For each quality, they will ask the same question, e.g. 'Do you think "intelligence" is a) very important, b) important, c) not very important, d) unimportant?'
- The students from this group go round the class, asking their questions. The results of the survey can then be reported back to the whole class. The whole activity can be carried out during parts of two or three lessons. The writing of the questionnaire and analysis of results can be done as homework by the group of students involved.

STUDY SECTION

Writing skills

- Draw students' attention to the formal language used in the report, and the linking words such as *in addition to*, *as well as*, *moreover*, *however*.

> *Answers*: **a** making a successful career **b** establishes good relations with **c** act a little impulsively **d** reacts negatively **e** to reach the most senior level

- Discuss reports such as this one. Who do they think wrote it? Do they think Julia read it? What is the purpose of reports like this? Has anyone in the class had to write this type of report?

Self-Check

> *Answers*: **1** of **2** with **3** with **4** should **5** is going to **6** to **7** has visited **8** might **9** were **10** was **11** am **12** are

4   WHO NEEDS FRIENDS LIKE THIS?

Overview of the unit

Lead-in: Cartoon-style story about a
so-called 'best' friend

Reading: Letter to an advice column of a
magazine ('How can I get my friend to
move out of my flat?')
Comprehension work

Language study: 1
● vocabulary (mate, friend, acquaintance,
etc.)*
● 'Am I selfish?' and 'Am I being selfish?'*
● word stress (the record; to record)

Role play: Asking a friend if you can stay
with him/her for a few days

Complete the dialogue: Asking a favour:
'Can you put me up for a few nights?'

Language study: 2
● different ways of asking favours (formal
and informal)*
● reporting requests*
● changing reported speech into direct
speech

Listen to the dialogue

Listening: Interviews with three people who
talk about the importance of friends to
them
Comprehension work

STUDY SECTION:
Writing: Sequencing sentences within
paragraphs and completing a reply from a
magazine 'problem page'
Self-Check: items marked * are included
here

Writing: Complete a summary of the
interviews

Lead-in

Read the text aloud yourself, with expression.
Then, get one or two students to read it aloud,
paying special attention to stress and intonation to
convey the man's feelings. Ask students to
explain the meaning of 'that was the last straw'
(i.e. . . . the last straw that broke the camel's
back).

Questions

Discuss questions 1 and 2 with the whole class,
then get students to do questions 3 and 4 in
small groups. After this lead-in, either go on to
the reading text which follows or develop the
more general theme of friendship and do the
Listening and Writing sections at the end of the
unit next.

Reading and comprehension work

Lots of different types of magazines have advice columns. Ask students what sort of problems people write about in different magazines, e.g. women's magazines, teenagers' magazines, music magazines, gardening magazines. Now go on to read the letter from Peter, and allow students sufficient time to think of questions to ask each other about the text. The *Ask and answer* work can then be done in groups or as a class activity.

Interpretation

Question 2 could develop into a short role play between Peter and his friend, which will prepare students for the *Role play* section which comes later in the unit.

Discussion

Question 2 relates back to the lead-in questions 3 and 4. This time, discuss the limits to friendship with the whole class.

Role play

Students work on the role play in pairs. Encourage the pairs to make slight alterations to the situation so that each role play is different, e.g. **A** has just moved to a new town because of his/her job; **B** often works at night and so needs to sleep during the day.

Language study: 1

Vocabulary study

As you check the exercise, ask students to make sentences containing some of the words so that they see if they can use them appropriately.

> *Answers:* **1** a **2** d **3** c **4** f **5** e
> **6** i **7** b **8** h **9** g

Describing behaviour

Teacher's reference: *A Communicative Grammar of English* **126**.
After discussing the pairs of examples here, ask students to look back at the last paragraph of Peter's letter (Do you think I am being selfish?) and to describe the behaviour of Peter and his friend.

What would you say in these situations?

> *Example answers:* **1** You're not being very helpful. **2** You're rather arrogant. **3** However, you're also very kind. **4** You're being very arrogant. **5** You're being foolish. **6** You're being stupid.

The same word as noun → verb

Students can look up the words in their dictionaries to check the stress if they are uncertain. The stress changes in all except 3 5 6 9 10. Notice that other pronunciation changes may accompany the stress change, e.g. record (noun)/ ˈrekɔːd/ (verb)/rɪˈkɔːd/

Dialogue

Complete the dialogue

> *Answers:* **1** c **2** f **3** i **4** n **5** k
> **6** h **7** a **8** l **9** o **10** g **11** d
> **12** b **13** m **14** e **15** j

Listening

Students listen to the dialogue, then close their books. Play the dialogue again, this time pausing for them to continue what is being said, e.g. 'Well, I was wondering (pause) ...'

Language study: 2

Mood and attitude: different ways of asking for favours

Answers: easy and relaxed –1, 4, 5
not so easy and relaxed – 2, 3, 6

After students have sorted out the examples into the two broad categories, get them to suggest how to respond to these requests (both agreeing and refusing to do the favour), e.g. Yes, of course/No, I'm afraid not (+ reason).

Asking favours

Students work in pairs, asking favours and responding. Encourage them to expand the request by prefacing it with some comment/explanation such as 'I was wondering if you could do me a favour' or 'My car won't start and I've got to meet my aunt at the station in half an hour'.

Ways of reporting requests

Suggested answers: **1** Can you lend me your car? **2** Can I keep it for a few days? **3** Could I have an extra set of keys in case my girlfriend wants to use it?

Report the requests

Suggested answers: **1** me to help him with his homework **2** for the answer to question 2 **3** if I had got a dictionary **4** me to explain the word 'tiny' **5** me to give him another word that means the same thing **6** if I would mind writing an essay for him in English **7** if he could use my phone **8** if I had got a pen because he might need it to write down some information **9** if I had got an umbrella he could borrow **10** if I could phone for a taxi for him **11** me for some money for the taxi **12** if I would mind helping him tomorrow as well.

Reporting what people say

Suggested answers: **1** I'll leave as soon as I find another place. **2** I'd like to think about it for a while. **3** Can you lend me some money? **4** How much do you need? **5** I'll pay it back in a few days. **6** I'm sorry I haven't paid the money back yet. **7** I completely forgot about it. **8** Please give me a few more days.

Listening

Questions

Students look at the pictures of Martin, Jean and Robert, and guess what their answers were to the three questions. Then, as they listen to the cassette, they can see if their guesses were right. As a follow-up, students can work in groups of 3 or 4, asking each other the same questions.

Writing summaries

This can be done for homework or in pairs in class. With weaker classes, it may be helpful to do the exercise as a whole class, building up the complete summary on the board.

STUDY SECTION

Writing skills

Answers: d c a b   f j i g k e h

Self-Check

Answers: **1** friends **2** if he could borrow **3** Can you lend me yours? **4** very careless **5** colleagues **6** Would it be possible to borrow your car? **7** I'm being difficult **8** I was wondering if I could borrow your car this evening.

5 SUCCESS AND FAILURE

Overview of the unit

```
┌─────────────────────────────────────────┐
│ Lead-in: Cartoon-style story of a self-  │
│          sufficient lifestyle            │
└─────────────────────────────────────────┘
              │
┌─────────────────────────────────────────┐      ┌──────────────────────────────────────────┐
│ Reading: What is success?               │      │ Language study: 1                          │
│ Comprehension work                      │──────│ ● vocabulary (stumble, stagger, etc.)*     │
└─────────────────────────────────────────┘      │ ● 'He went into the kitchen and drank      │
                                                  │   his coffee' and 'He went into the kitchen,│
                                                  │   drinking his coffee.'*                   │
                                                  │ ● 'When James came back, Joyce got         │
                                                  │   up' and 'When James came back, Joyce     │
                                                  │   had got up.'*                            │
                                                  └──────────────────────────────────────────┘

                                                  ┌──────────────────────────────────────────┐
                                                  │ Language study: 2                          │
┌─────────────────────────────────────────┐      │ ● giving definite and cautious assurances* │
│ Complete the dialogue: Herr Kohler phones│──────│ ● I hope so/I hope not*                     │
│ Hugh about the delivery of his goods    │      │ ● words and their forms (deliver/delivery,  │
└─────────────────────────────────────────┘      │   etc.)*                                    │
              │                                   │ ● word stress (tracksuit, sportscar etc)   │
┌─────────────────────────────────────────┐      └──────────────────────────────────────────┘
│ Listening: Full dialogue between Herr    │
│ Kohler and Hugh                         │      ┌──────────────────────────────────────────┐
└─────────────────────────────────────────┘      │ STUDY SECTION                              │
              │                                   │ Writing: Completing a letter with          │
┌─────────────────────────────────────────┐      │   prepositions and modifiers and then      │
│ What would you say in these situations? │      │   replying to this letter from a penfriend │
│ (using expressions from the dialogue)   │      │ Self-Check: items marked * are included    │
└─────────────────────────────────────────┘      │   here                                     │
                                                  └──────────────────────────────────────────┘
```

Lead-in

● Before using the book, write on the board:

Success

Ask students to note down everything that comes to mind when they think of success. Give them about 2 minutes to work on this individually. Then, in pairs, students can compare their notes. This can lead into a class discussion of success and failure, which could include a discussion of cultural differences, e.g. what do students think British people regard as symbols of success?

● Turn to the lead-in, and read the text aloud yourself.

● Ask students to cover the text and tell you what they remember about this man. If necessary, prompt them with questions, e.g.

'Where does he live? Where does he get his money from?'

● Students discuss the answers to the questions in groups of 3 or 4. At the end, they may be interested to find out how many of their class would like to live like this – have a quick show of hands.

Reading

● Set a time limit (4 minutes) and ask students to read this for the main facts, ignoring details and words they do not understand.

● Ask students to close their books. Write on the board:

James Hugh

● Ask the class to tell you everything they can remember about James and Hugh. Make notes on the board of their main points. They will probably find that, as a class, they have remembered a lot! Then go on to the *Comprehension* questions.

Comprehension

Encourage students to refer back to the text and quote from it in order to support and illustrate their answers.

Interpretation

● Working in pairs, students describe either a typical day in the life of James or a typical day in the life of Hugh. Tell them they can make notes if they wish. As the pairs are working, go round and listen to check if they are using present simple forms correctly for describing habits. If they are making mistakes, do some remedial work on this afterwards.
● The pairs then report back to the class, using their notes for reference if they want to, but not reading aloud a complete written text.

Which is the best description?

> *Answers:* **1** best describes the way James felt about Hugh. **a** 2 **b** 1 **c** 3

● If some of the words (*envy, contempt, resent*) are new to the class, ask them to make up some more sentences using these words to check that they can use them appropriately.
● Ask students how they would describe the way Hugh feels about James. If necessary, write the following words on the board to start them thinking.

contempt   jealous   respect   sympathy
pity tolerate   irritating

Language study: 1
Vocabulary study

With the words in 1 to 6, students will find it helpful to look at these words in the text as they work through the matching exercise.
7 to 12 can be done in pairs. Then, the pairs can make up sentences containing these words.

> *Answers:* **1** d **2** b **3** a **4** f **5** e
> **6** c **7** i **8** k **9** j **10** g **11** l **12** h
> Irregular past form is *creep – crept*.

Complete the sentences

This could be set for homework. Then, in the next lesson, ask students to read out some of their own sentences using these verbs.

> *Answers:* **1** strolled **2** limping
> **3** stumbled **4** crawled **5** crept
> **6** lurched

What is the difference in meaning?

Working in pairs, students discuss the sentences. Check that they have all worked out that sentences 1a and 2a show that both actions happened at the same time and sentences 1b and 2b show that one action happened before the other. Then, ask them to write down another pair of sentences, using these two structures (the sentences need not be based on the text).

Make one sentence

Tell the class that the six sentences form a sequence based on the text. Do the exercise with the class, paying particular attention to stress and intonation patterns as students read the sentences aloud.

> *Answers*: **1** Hugh woke up, feeling terrible. **2** He sat in the kitchen, drinking his coffee. **3** He drank his coffee, thinking about the day ahead. **4** James came back from his run, feeling good. **5** Mandy lay in bed, holding a big teddy bear. **6** James had a shower, singing 'Oh what a wonderful morning!'

What is the difference in meaning?

● Allow sufficient time for students to study the sentences before asking which action happened first.

> *Answers*: **1a** Joyce got up. **1b** James came back. **2a** The alarm went off. **2b** Hugh woke up.

● Ask them to think back to what happened at the beginning of the lesson/school day and have them make statements, using the same structures. Give an example yourself first – I was late and lessons had started when I got to school./The school bell rang and the pupils went into their classrooms.

What do you think had happened?

> *Possible answers*: **1** When I looked out of the window, I realized it had got dark. **2** My money had been stolen/had gone. **3** Hugh and Helen had quarrelled. **4** Hugh had had too much to drink the night before. **5** Hugh had already left when I phoned yesterday morning.

Dialogue

Complete the dialogue

● Students read through the dialogue silently, guessing the missing words/phrases and making a note of them, but *not* looking at the list of missing words/phrases.
● In pairs, students read through the dialogue again, this time checking their ideas with the list

of missing words/phrases. When they have finished, they can read the dialogue aloud in their pairs.
If students have suggested alternative words/phrases which are not listed, discuss these with the whole class.
Language study: 2 could be introduced at this point, before students listen to the dialogue. Their attention will then be focused on the language of assurances.

> *Answers*: **1** d **2** n **3** g **4** a **5** i **6** e **7** m **8** k **9** o **10** h **11** l **12** b **13** j **14** c **15** f

Listening

● As the students listen for the first time, ask them to note down the difference (half the order will be delivered by the 24th and the rest a week later).
● Ask the students to take the part of Hugh as you play the cassette again. This time, pause the cassette before each of Hugh's speeches, and ask students to continue. Encourage them to respond appropriately, without worrying about saying exactly what is on the cassette.

What would you say in these situations?

● Students work in pairs, referring back to the written dialogue to find the phrases.
● Check the answers with the whole class.
● Ask students if they know any other phrases which mean roughly the same, and discuss these, e.g. *you can depend on us* means almost the same as *you can count on us*, but is slightly more formal.

> *Answers*: **1** put him through **2** I'll come straight to the point **3** you can count on me to do my very best **4** there's no need to worry

Language study: 2

Assurances: definite and not so definite

- Have students work in pairs, discussing the six sentences, before checking them.

> *Answers*: Herr Kohler would probably be satisfied with 2, 3 and 6.

- Draw students' attention to the language which does not commit the speaker (*we're doing our best* and *we can't foresee*) and the function of modals (*should*).

Definite assurances/Cautious assurances

- Do these exercises orally, paying particular attention to stress and intonation.
- After going through both exercises with the whole class, have students work in pairs, selecting one of the situations and creating the full conversation.

I hope so/I hope not

Students work in pairs. First, Student **A** has his book open and student **B** closes his book. Student **A** reads out the sentences, and **B** listens and responds with 'I hope so'/'I hope not'. Then students change roles, and Student **B** reads out the sentences but in a different order.

> *Answers*: **1** I hope not. **2** I hope so. **3** I hope so. **4** I hope not. **5** I hope not. **6** I hope so.

Words and their forms

This can be set as homework, and students allowed to refer to good monolingual dictionaries if they wish.

> *Answers*: **1** delivery **2** assurance **3** dependent **4** solution **5** understanding **6** relieved **7** celebration **8** completion **9** payment **10** receipt **11** engagement **12** speciality/specialization **13** comfortable **14** noticeable **15** entertainment

Compound words (noun + noun)

All these examples illustrate the general rule that compound nouns are generally stressed on the first element but with a strong secondary stress on the second element, e.g. 'track ˌsuit elec'tronics engin,eer

STUDY SECTION

Writing skills

Introduce this in class, by asking students if they have any penfriends. Ask them what they would write about in a first letter to a penfriend. Then, explain that this letter is a reply to an advertisement for a penfriend. Draw their attention to the way this letter is divided into paragraphs and remind them to write in paragraphs when answering part 2 of the exercise.

> *Answers*: **1** 1i **2** a **3** f **4** d **5** g **6** h **7** k **8** l **9** b **10** c **11** e **12** j

Self-Check

> *Answers*: **1** had gone **2** slipped **3** speciality **4** had seen **5** carrying **6** We'll **7** so **8** and bought **9** uncomfortable **10** strolled **11** holding **12** and arrested

6 VOICES FROM NOWHERE

Overview of the unit

Lead-in: Describing and speculating about a picture of a house

Reading: The story of a haunted house
Comprehension work

Discussion: Do you think this house is haunted?

Complete the dialogue: A neighbour tells Mrs Long something about the history of the house

Language study: 1
- assumptions and opinions (must have/supposed to have/should have)*
- having things done (they had the house redecorated)*

- reacting to what people say*

Listening: Full dialogue between neighbour and Mrs Long

Role play: Take the part of the neighbour

Reading: Who said what? Two psychologists give their opinions about ghosts
Comprehension work

Language study: 2
- the language of belief and disbelief (accept/reject it, sceptical about, etc.)*
- word stress (explain; explanation)

Writing: A summary of why the psychologists disagree

Reading: A ghost is exorcised
Sort out the jumbled text

Listening: A journalist tells a strange story that happened to him

STUDY SECTION
Writing: Completing a report about a house for sale and writing an advertisement for it
Self-Check: items marked * are included here

Lead-in

- Encourage students to speculate as much as possible about the picture by asking detailed questions to follow up each of the four questions given.
- Using *would have to be* when answering question 4 will prepare the students for the language work which comes later in this unit. They can work in pairs, listing all the things which would have to be done. Then there can be a reporting-back session with the whole class.
- Ask the students to look at the title of the unit (*Voices From Nowhere*) and the picture. Can they predict what the text is going to be about in this unit? They will probably guess that it is about 'ghosts' or 'unnatural happenings'. You may find that there is a 'strange happening' in the news at the moment which students can discuss and comment on.

Reading/True or false?

- Read the first paragraph of the text aloud, students following in their books. Then ask them to tell you the advantages and disadvantages of the house and to guess what the 'terrible things' were which happened.
- Before continuing the reading, have students look at the *True or false* section. Read the statements aloud. Students then read the rest of the text silently, and decide if these statements are true or false.
- Check the answers with the whole class, getting students to read aloud the parts of the text which support their answers.

Answers: **1** T **2** T **3** F **4** T **5** F **6** T

Vocabulary

- Students can do the exercise in pairs.

Answers: **1** the creeps **2** nightmares **3** to find someone guilty **4** to suspect **5** dismembered **6** ghosts **7** are superstitious **8** hysterical

- Select four or five of these words, and have students use them in their own statements. For example, ask students: 'What gives you the creeps?' ('Walking down a dark street at night gives me the creeps.')

Discussion

Students work in groups of 3 or 4 discussing this story and exchanging opinions.
You may find that some students have similar stories or experiences to relate. This will give them good practice in story-telling and speaking in 'chunks' of language. After a student has told his story to the class, have another student re-tell it. (This is an effective way of showing if the narrator has communicated successfully and if the re-teller has understood and remembered successfully.)

Dialogue

- Students read through the dialogue silently to get a general idea of the whole conversation. Ask them what Mrs Long learns from the neighbour.
- In pairs, students read the dialogue again, noting down their suggestions for the missing words or phrases. Then they can look at the list of missing words and fit them in. After this, they can read the dialogue aloud in pairs.
- Discuss with the whole class any of their suggested words or phrases which are different from the ones listed. Decide if their alternatives are equally appropriate and acceptable.

Answers: **1** d **2** n **3** j **4** e **5** l **6** a **7** m **8** i **9** b **10** k **11** g **12** c **13** h **14** f

Listening

- During the first listening, students note down the new information from the neighbour. (Gordon Taplow seemed a nice man. He had invited her in for a cup of tea, but she never went because she was always too busy.)
- Play the cassette again and this time ask students to listen to the *way* the women speak, especially

their stress and intonation. How does it compare with the way the students read the dialogue in their pairs? After students have discussed this, play the cassette again and have them repeat some of the exchanges, e.g.

(i) *Mrs Long*: Do you mind if I ask you something?
   Neighbour: No, of course not. Go ahead.
(ii) *Mrs Long*: What are you talking about?
   Neighbour: Those terrible murders that happened here more than twenty years ago.
   Mrs Long: Murders? What murders?
   Neighbour: But I thought you knew!

Take the part of the neighbour

One procedure is as follows:
● Read the part of Mrs Long yourself with one student playing the part of the neighbour (the student should have his/her book closed). It is important that you respond appropriately to what the 'neighbour' says, improvising on the dialogue when necessary.
● Students then do the same in pairs. The student taking the role of the neighbour closes his/her book. The other student has his/her book open, but makes changes according to what the neighbour says.

Language study: 1

What is the difference in meaning?

Students work in small groups of 3 or 4, discussing the examples.

> *Answers*: **1** c   **2** a   **3** b

Expressing assumptions and other people's opinions

● Read the examples aloud, and discuss them with the class.
● Students do the exercise as a pair activity. Student **A** has the book open, and Student **B** closes his book. Student **A** reads out sentences 1–4 and **B** listens and responds. Then the roles

are reversed for sentences 5–8.

> *Answers*: **1** It must be raining.   **2** It is supposed to get very hot in Texas in summer.   **3** Dallas is supposed to be very expensive.   **4** He must be from Texas.   **5** Professor Hardhead's lecture yesterday is supposed to have been very interesting.   **6** Laura Longlegs must have felt tired afterwards.   **7** The race is supposed to have been very exciting.   **8** He must have been mad/crazy.

What is the difference in meaning?

● Ask students to look back at the lead-in picture, and make statements about the things the new owners 'had done', e.g. 'They had the rooms decorated.'
● Look at the example sentences, and discuss them with the whole class.

> *Answer*: We had the house redecorated.

Having things done

This can be done in the same way as the exercise *Expressing assumptions and other people's opinions*.
● Students work in pairs, one having the book open to read the prompts and the other having the book closed and responding to the prompts. Encourage the students to change the order of the prompts.
● After working through the exercise, give further practice in saying what *will/is going to be done* by asking students, in pairs, to write down six more things which will be done tomorrow.
● Then, two pairs come together to form groups of 4 students. Each pair tells the other pair about the things they are going to have done tomorrow.

Reacting to things people say

● Ask students to cover up a)–j). Read aloud each statement 1–10, getting students to react with appropriate responses.
● Students then look at a)–j) and see if any of

these responses are the same as the ones they suggested. Go through the exercise again, matching the prompts and the given responses.
- Ask each student to think of three statements giving good, bad or surprising news. Then students work in pairs, one student giving three pieces of news and the other student reacting appropriately.

Reading

Who said what?

- Tell the class that Dr Holborn and Mr Arthur are not having a conversation, i.e. they are not answering each other. Each of them is making a separate, fairly long, speech.
- Begin each sequence with the whole class (sentence 1 followed by sentence 3; sentence 2 followed by sentence 5). Then, let students work in pairs completing the sequences. Advise them to complete Jill's speech first. They should then read them aloud (still working in pairs) to check that they are happy with their answers.
- Ask students what they think of these two opinions. Which do they agree with? Do they know of any other 'strange happenings' which have later been explained when a deception was discovered?

> *Answers*: Jill Holborn: 1, 3, 4, 7, 9, 11, 13, 14, 16. James Arthur: 2, 5, 6, 8, 10, 12, 15.

Give the full meaning

This can be set as homework or done in class in pairs.

> *Answers*: sentence 6: as delusions or fakes
> sentence 7: stories like 'Voices from nowhere'
> sentence 11: the man with a weak heart
> sentence 12: such as the Longs' case
> sentence 15: investigate a little further before we come to any definite conclusion
> sentence 16: the time he regretted his decision

Explain

In these 'explanation' tasks, students should be given sufficient time to think out what they want to say, and then to give a full answer, speaking in a connected sequence of sentences. One procedure is:
- Students work in groups of 3. Each student takes one of the three tasks and is given time to think about it, and make notes.
- Then each student in the group gives an explanation to the other two members of the group, who can ask questions at the end of the explanation if they want to.

Writing summaries

This can be set as homework or done with the whole class, building up the summary on the board. The main points to include are: 'the readiness to believe such stories is unscientific and harmful' versus 'it is important to keep an open mind in the search for truth because the known laws of science may not be able to explain everything'.
Notice that *Language study: 2* relates to the texts about these two psychologists and could follow on from this task.

Find the story

- Students work in pairs, sorting out the text.
- Ask questions to check comprehension, e.g. 'Where do Prince and Princess Michael of Kent live?' (Near Stroud.) 'When was the blacksmith hanged?' (300 years ago.) 'Did the priests succeed in getting rid of the ghost?' (We don't know.)

> *Answers*: c b e d a

Language study: 2

Vocabulary study

- Allow students sufficient time to read and think about the sentences before checking the exercise with the whole class.

Answers: **1** d **2** c **3** b **4** g **5** f **6** e **7** a

- Ask the students to give their own opinions about ghosts, the supernatural or some strange 'happening' that is in the news at the moment. Encourage them to use the language of belief and disbelief, together with the language of expressing opinions which occurs here and in the reading text (*I sincerely believe that .../I'm sceptical about .../Personally, ... /My view is that ...*).

Explain – explanation

All the examples illustrate the rule that the noun has the stress on the penultimate syllable (–'ation). Draw students' attention to changes in spelling in the first two examples.

Expressing beliefs and disbeliefs

Students can work in groups of 3 or 4, expressing their opinions. Encourage them to agree and disagree (politely) with each other.

Listening

- Play the whole cassette first for gist comprehension. Then look at the questions with the whole class, and see if the students can answer some of them.
- Replay the cassette, pausing when necessary, and elicit answers to all the questions.
- Play the cassette again, asking students to listen for any other information. Then, in pairs, students make up three more questions about the story. The pairs then come together in groups of 4, and ask each other their questions.

- Finally, have the students re-tell the story as a 'chain' exercise, i.e. Student **A** begins the narrative and stopps after one or two sentences for Student **B** to continue, and so on. Encourage students to use linking devices to make the story flow, e.g. *The next thing that happened was .../As soon as .../Before—ing ...*

Answers: **1** Frankfurt **2** 6 o'clock on a Saturday evening **3** The phone rang but there was nobody there when he answered it. This happened twice. **4** Yes. He was strange and pale and he never spoke.

STUDY SECTION

Writing skills

- Introduce the task in class. Ask students to read the memorandum quickly to find out: (i) What have the Longs decided to do about the house? (Sell it.) (ii) What does Mr Hill want Mr Woolley to do? (Give a report on his visit and advise on the wording of the advertisement.) Then ask students (iii) Do you think Mr Hill and Mr Woolley are of equal status at work? – Why/Why not? (Mr Hill is of higher status.) (iv) What 'special qualities' might be mentioned to attract a buyer looking for an unusual residence? (The house has its own ghost.)
- Students can complete the report for homework, using information from the texts in the unit and their own imagination.
- If suitable for your class, this could lead into further study of advertisements (especially house advertisements) or a role play between the estate agent and a potential buyer.

Self-Check

Answers: **1** Oh? I'm glad to hear that. **2** Really? How interesting. **3** had it redecorated **4** repaired the windows **5** was supposed to **6** sceptical **7** reject **8** must **9** had a ghost exorcized **10** should **11** have the garden dug up

7 SPORT AND VIOLENCE

Overview of the Unit

Lead-in: Describing and discussing a picture of a boxing match

Reading: Newspaper article about a fight between football fans
Comprehension work

Language study: 1
- it must have/might have happened*
- 'Despite' and 'although'*
- prepositions*
- pronunciation of 'ou' (count; should)

Find the dialogue: Inviting a friend to a volleyball match

Language study: 2
- agreeing/disagreeing with someone and giving your own reasons/comments*
- vocabulary (tennis, football, etc.)

Listening:
Full dialogue

Role play:
Persuading a friend to go to a film, etc. with you

Writing: Completing a summary

STUDY SECTION
Writing: Completing a letter to a newspaper using linking constructions, and then replying to this letter
Self-Check: items marked * are included here

Lead in/Questions

- Question 1 encourages students to develop a complete 'picture-in-words' of the boxing match. Use the questions given and add more of your own, e.g. 'How do you think the two boxers are feeling? What do you think the commentator is saying?
- From describing the picture and their reactions to it, students move on to discuss other sports. Further areas of vocabulary can be developed, e.g. sounds (*cheer*, *shout*, *boo*, *clap*, etc.) or sports and where they take place (*boxing/ring*, *tennis/court*, *ice-skating/rink*, etc.)

Listening

- Stop the cassette after each of the three speakers, and ask the appropriate questions.
- Play all the interviews again, and ask further questions to encourage students to speculate about the speakers, e.g. 'How old do you think each speaker is? What impression do you have of each speaker?' (job, appearance, personality).

Answers: **1** Why anyone should go to a boxing match. **2** Through her boyfriend.
3 Possibly that she likens it to chess.
4 Probably not, because he feels strongly that it is brutal.

Reading/Interpretation

- Use question 1 from the *Interpretation* section as a pre-question, and ask students to read through the text quickly to find the answer.
- Go on to more intensive reading of the text and answer questions 2 and 3 from the *Interpretation* section.
- Develop the discussion by asking further questions, e.g. 'What else could the writer have done at the time? What would you have done? Have you ever been in a similar situation?' (as an onlooker? participant?) 'If so, what did you do?'

Vocabulary

> *Answers:* **1** b **2** c **3** a **4** a
> **5** a **6** c

Comprehension

Read the four questions aloud, then give the class time to look at the text again, with these questions in mind. An alternative is to allocate one question to each student, so that they concentrate on one aspect, not all four.
- Then students close their books and give their answers in their own words. Allow individual students sufficient time to answer fully in a connected sequence of sentences. If it is practical, you could record their answers on tape, then replay them later for correction of any major errors and follow-up work.

Language study: 1

What is the difference in meaning?

Students discuss the sentences, working in pairs. Then ask them if they can remember which sentence was used in the reading text. (2). 'Why would sentence (2) be more appropriate?' (Because the writer could not see clearly and, in a café, there would be a number of different objects which could have been thrown.) Ask the class to think of a situation in which sentence (1) would be used. (The speaker can see a broken ashtray on the floor, or knows that the ashtray was the only object around at the time.)

Using 'must have ...' or 'might have ...'

Read the examples with the class. Then have students close their books. Read aloud each of the prompts and ask students to respond, using *must have* or *might have*. This will provide listening comprehension practice, rather than reading practice.

> *Answers:* **1** must **2** might **3** might
> **4** must **5** must **6** must **7** must
> **8** might

'Despite' ... or 'Although ...'?

Working in small groups of 3 or 4, students study and discuss the examples. The exercise can be set as homework, after checking that all the students have worked out that *although* is used with a verb phrase and *despite* with a noun phrase.

> *Answers:* **1** Although **2** Despite
> **3** Despite **4** Although
> **5** Although **6** Despite **7** Despite
> **8** Although

Review of basic prepositions

Explain to the class that the eight sentences form a sequence of events based on the reading text.

> *Answers:* **1** at **2** on **3** to
> **4** between **5** out **6** at **7** by
> **8** with

How is 'ou' pronounced?

Students can look up the words in their dictionaries if they are unsure of the pronunciation.
Answers 1 should 2 sound 3 thought 4 mouth 5 out 6 cough
Give the students time to think about the pronunciation of the two sentences before reading them aloud.

Dialogue

Find the dialogue

This section and the following sections develop the theme of invitations – issuing an invitation, persuading someone to accept, accepting or declining an invitation.

- Students work in pairs to find the dialogue, and then read it aloud in their pairs.
- Then have students close their books. Read aloud sentences 1–9 yourself, asking students to respond spontaneously. Tell them that it does not matter if they do not give the same responses as in the book, but they should respond appropriately. Notice that you may have to adapt your 'part' to accommodate what the students say.
- Finally, in pairs, the students can do the same activity. One student closes his book and the other has his book open, using sentences 1–9 as a guide, but adapting them when necessary.

Writing

This can be given as homework or done individually in class. If students do it in class, they can exchange books with their neighbour when they have finished, and read each other's summaries. Encourage them to co-operate in correction of any errors in their work.

Listening

> *Answer:* The extra information is that **B** pays the £5 for the ticket.

After playing the cassette once for students to find the extra information, play it again and pause it appropriately for students to complete what the speaker is saying, for example:

A: I've got two tickets for a volleyball match this evening. Why ... (*pause tape*)

B: No, thanks. I'm not very ... (*pause tape*) etc.

Role play

Some classes will find it helpful if the work in *More than just agreement or disagreement* in *Language study: 2* is done before the role play, so that they can use this language confidently in their role plays.

If possible, bring copies of *What's On* or the Entertainment Guide from a newspaper, and begin by revising the vocabulary of entertainment. If you cannot obtain texts in English, notice that texts in the mother tongue can also be used here, if you set up a situation in which students are inviting an English-speaking visitor to an event in their own town.

The realia can then be used in the role play, student **A** selecting an event and inviting **B** to come along. The pairs can then change roles, and repeat the role play using a different event.

Language study: 2

More than just agreement or disagreement

- In pairs, students read aloud the examples, paying attention to stress and intonation.
- Ask the class to suggest other comments which speakers **B** and **C** could make after their initial agreement or disagreement.

Giving your own opinions

Students work in pairs. Student **A** (book open) reads sentences 1–4 in any order and student **B** (book closed) responds. Then, roles are reversed for sentences 5–8.

Additional comments

- Still in pairs, students work together matching the six additions to the comments, and discussing if they agree with them.

> Answers: **a** 7 **b** 2 **c** 6 **d** 3 **e** 4
> **f** 8

- Students can then suggest additional comments for the two remaining examples (1, 5).

Vocabulary study: sport

For the last part of the exercise students can work in groups of 3 or 4, listing the words and phrases connected with a sport of their own choice.

> *Answers:* **1** tennis (clues – game, serves, set) **2** football (clues – pass, crossed, put the ball in the net, header) **3** boxing (clues – floored, ninth round, technical knockout, a good right/left)

What is it?

Students work in groups of 3 or 4, preparing a description of a particular sport. Let the groups refer to dictionaries if they wish to, and ask for your help in describing equipment or rules in English.

> *Answer:* badminton

STUDY SECTION

Writing skills

When presenting this in class, ask students if they have ever written a letter to a newspaper (or to a radio/TV station). If so, what was it about? Was it answered/published? What sort of things do they feel strongly enough about to write such a letter?

> *Answers:* **1** c **2** e **3** g **4** d **5** b **6** f
> **7** a

Self-Check

After students have done this exercise, it can be used to start a discussion on the topic of football violence. Is this a particularly British problem? Why does it happen? How could it be stopped?

> *Answers:* **1** between **2** at **3** might
> **4** on **5** with **6** must **7** don't
> **8** although **9** Despite **10** out
> **11** Neither

8 YOUTH AND EXPERIENCE

Overview of the unit

Lead-in: Discussion about what you hope to have done before you reach the age of 70

Reading: Things I wish I'd known at 18 – an article by Sir Anton Dolin
Comprehension work

Language study: 1
- I wish I had/had had children*
- I would like to have/to have had children*
- future in the past (He knew he was going to/would . . .)*

Reading
1 The first part of a story based on an event that happened in New York in 1954
Comprehension work
2 The second part of the story (explain what had happened/was going to happen)
Comprehension work

Language study: 2
- vocabulary (mutter, groan, etc.)*
- stress and meaning (You know how I feel about you)

Writing: The full story

STUDY SECTION
Writing: Complete a speech of welcome and then prepare (in writing) a speech to welcome a visiting speaker to an English-speaking society
Self-Check: items marked * are included here

Lead-in

How you develop the lead-in discussion will depend on the age of the majority of your class. Many students will feel more relaxed discussing the questions in small groups rather than with the whole class.

Question 2 (How old is 'old' today?) can lead to a more general discussion, e.g. how 'old' people are regarded and treated in different societies, what age people retire/should retire.

Reading

This text can be handled as a 'jigsaw' reading activity, as follows:

• Read the introduction aloud to the class and check comprehension ('Is Anton Dolin still alive? Who was he?')

• Divide the class into three groups, and have each group read (silently) one section of the text only – Group 1 reads paragraphs 1–3; Group 2 reads paragraphs 4–6; Group 3 reads paragraphs 7–9.

• Write on the board

*childhood   young man   later life
personality   regrets*

• Students then tell the class what they have found out about Anton Dolin. Make notes under each heading as they are reporting back.
Give the class time to read through the whole text (silently) before going on.

True or false?

Students can do the exercise working in pairs. It is important that they read out the section of the text which supports their answers.

> *Answers:* **1** F **2** T **3** F **4** F **5** T
> **6** T **7** T **8** F

Comprehension

Give students sufficient time to refer back to the text and formulate their answers. Then, have them work in groups of 3 or 4, explaining and describing as fully as possible.

Vocabulary

> *Answers:* **1** b **2** c **3** c **4** b

After doing the exercise and checking the answers, ask students to suggest suitable words for some of the alternatives, e.g. someone with a good education (*well-educated*), foolish with money (*extravagant/a spendthrift*).

Language study: 1

Discuss the differences

Students work in groups of 3 or 4 discussing the examples and answering the questions.

> Answers: **1** b and d **2** c **3** a. The
> speaker is sorry he/she has not got children.

Using 'wish' and 'would like'

This could be set as homework.

> *Answers:* **1** hadn't been **2** hadn't
> lost **3** have been **4** have had **5** have
> (got/been) **6** had done

What about you?

Here the students have an opportunity to use the language more freely and talk about themselves, so allow sufficient time for thought beforehand and for the discussion itself.

The future in the past

Discuss the examples with the whole class. Then ask students to make further examples using these prompts on the board.

I wish I had known	when I began this course	that. . .
I would like to have known	ten years ago last year	

Using the future in the past

Have one of the students read the introduction and example aloud. Then do the first two questions with the whole class. After this, students work in pairs on the last four questions, and then refer back to the text to find the answers.

What about you?

Give students a few minutes to think of three things. Then, they work in groups of 3 or 4, telling each other of their three things. The emphasis here is on both fluency and accuracy, so encourage self- and peer-correction in the groups if mistakes are made.

Reading

If possible, plan to cover the last section of the unit (from *Reading* onwards) in consecutive lessons, so that students do not lose the momentum of the story.
Write on the board

Mary   Bill

Tell students to read the text quickly to gain a general impression of Mary and Bill and their relationship. Then, discuss their impressions. Note down their ideas on the board, then look at these notes again after the *Explain* activity to see if their first impressions have changed.

Comprehension and interpretation

Students work in groups of 3 or 4, reading the text and answering the questions. Encourage them to discuss different possible answers and interpretations, giving reasons for their points of view.

Explain

This revises the past perfect and *going to*. Encourage students to create as many sentences as they can for each example. The exercise could be set as homework, and then checked orally in class in the next lesson.

Vocabulary

Students can do this in groups of 3 or 4, writing down their answers. Go round and check their answers as they are working.

Possible answers: **1** sentence 4: She had arranged to meet Steve. **2** sentence 12: They had reached a verdict. **3** sentence 5: He was going to follow her. **4** sentence 12: He was going to be sentenced to death. **5** sentence 8: He was going to shoot her. **6** sentence 10: Bill had killed Mary. **7** sentence 11: They had buried Mary.

Writing

This can be set as homework.

Language study: 2

Vocabulary study

Have students cover the verbs and look at the definitions. Have individual students read aloud a), h) and j) and see if the class can supply these three words. Then let students look at the verbs and see if their suggestions are there. Have the class repeat all the verbs after you to practise pronunciation, then work through the whole exercise.

Answers: **1** i **2** g **3** e **4** h **5** a **6** c **7** d **8** j **9** b **10** f

The sentence completion exercise could be set as homework.

Possible answers: **1** muttered **2** murmured **3** whispered **4** groaned **5** screamed **6** stuttered **7** chatting/chattering **8** shouted **9** shouted or snarled

Understanding stress

● Have students repeat the sentences after you, and discuss their meanings.

Answers: **a** 2 **b** 3 **c** 4 **d** 1

• Have individual students say one of the four sentences aloud and the rest of the class listen then identify which sentence they have heard. If more practice is needed, students can continue the same activity in groups of 3 or 4.

Using stress

• Do the example (I'll always love you.) with the whole class, asking individual students to say the sentence for each of the four meanings.

> *Main stresses*: **1** always **2** you
> **3** I'll **4** love

• Students work in groups of 3 or 4 on the next four statements, using stress to convey different meanings.
• Finally, have the groups of 3 or 4 select one of the four sentences and write a short dialogue which includes it. Give them an example first:

A: Do you like our local wines?

B: I don't know – I haven't tried any yet. But I really like your *food*.

A: Do you? Most tourists think it's too spicy.

STUDY SECTION

Writing skills

• Ask students if any of them have had experience in making speeches in their mother tongue, e.g. at weddings, at work, in college or in societies to which they belong. If so, how do they prepare a speech? (Write notes? Write out the whole speech? Learn it by heart? Speak spontaneously?)

The example given is based on information from the entry for Jeffrey Archer in *Who's Who*. It is not necessary to spend a long time working through this entry, but you could do some work on abbreviations if your students are interested in this.

Abbreviations:

b born; *s* son; *m* married; *Educ* educated; *Sch* school; *Coll* college; *'blue'* (at Oxford and Cambridge universities) the right to wear a blue cap, scarf, etc.; awarded to a person who has represented the University in sports; *Pres* president; *OUAC* Oxford University Athletic Club; *Mem. GLC* Member of the Greater London Council; *MP (C)* Conservative Member of Parliament; *Mem. Exec.* Member of the Executive; *AAA* Amateur Athletics Association; *Chm* Chairman; *RFC* Rugby Football Club; *FRSA* Fellow of the Royal Society of Arts; *CCC* County Cricket Club; *MCC* Marylebone Cricket Club (the governing body of English cricket).

• Explain that in task 2 students are asked to write out the speech in English.
• Remind them that this is written language intended to be spoken, so they should read it aloud after they have written it in order to check that it 'reads' well. The class may enjoy hearing some of the speeches after they have been written.

> *Answers*: **1** d **2** a **3** i **4** g **5** h **6** e
> **7** c **8** f **9** b

Self-Check

> *Answers*: **1** had **2** shouting **3** whisper
> **4** giggling **5** had known **6** to have
> seen **7** to see

9   A HEALTHY LIFE

Overview of the unit

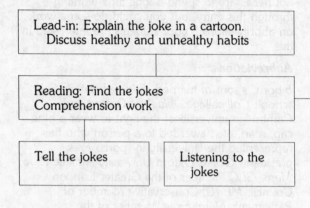

Lead-in: Explain the joke in a cartoon.
Discuss healthy and unhealthy habits

Reading: Find the jokes
Comprehension work

Tell the jokes

Listening to the jokes

Language study: 1
• vocabulary (ask, demand, inquire)*
• stress and meaning (What are you doing down there?)
• suggesting that things are easy to do (All you have to do is work hard)*

Reading: Interview with an expert on heart disease
Comprehension work

Language study: 2
• I used to do it/I'm used to doing it*
• 'consider' and 'regard'*
• the language of cause and effect*

STUDY SECTION
Writing: Writing about the members of a family in their letter of application to join a Twinning Association
Self-Check: items marked * are included here

Lead-in

Have students look at and read the cartoon. Ask them what their first reaction was. To smile? To feel angry? No reaction? Then go on to discuss the three questions. Question 3 (Not everybody would think this joke is funny. Explain why.) can lead into a wider discussion of different senses of humour. 'What makes you laugh'? 'What do you understand by 'the British sense of humour'?' (Perhaps show students a copy of *Punch* or *Private Eye* to illustrate two aspects of British humour.)

Discussion

Questions 1 and 2 can be treated as follows:
• Have one half of the class make a list of 'healthy habits' (with reasons) and the other half make a list of 'unhealthy habits' (with reasons).
• Discuss the two lists with the whole class. If the same habit occurs in both lists (e.g. jogging may occur in both), students must describe exactly why it can be healthy and unhealthy.
• Students work in groups of 3 or 4 discussing the quotations in question 3. Encourage them also to consider other sayings they can remember about 'a healthy life', e.g. An apple a day keeps the doctor away. Early to bed, early to rise, makes a man healthy, wealthy and wise.

Find the joke/Tell the joke

- First, look at the cartoon of the two sailors and encourage students to guess what is happening. Ask questions such as 'What nationality are they?/Where do you think they are?/What sort of place is it?/What time do you think it is?/What were they doing earlier in the evening?/What do you think they are doing now?/How do you think they are feeling?/What do you think is going to happen in the next few minutes?'
- Students work in pairs, sorting out the jokes and then reading them aloud to each other. They can then compare their reading with the readings of the jokes on cassette.
- Ask students which nationalities 'suffer' in the jokes told in their countries – English people often make jokes in which the Irish appear stupid or the Scots appear mean. Some students may even be able to tell a joke in English (though many jokes are difficult to translate).

> *Answers*: 1, 3, 6, 7, 10, 12, 13, 16,/ 2, 4, 5, 8, 9, 11, 14, 15.

Explain the words

> *Answers*: **1** *there* – in the pub **2** *there* – in the gutter **3** *that* – the fact that my father did all those things and yet he died a very poor man at the age of only 39. **4** *them* – all those things, i.e. avoid bad habits like drinking and smoking, get up early every morning, work at least ten hours a day and save *every penny*.

Language study: 1

Vocabulary study

In pairs, students discuss the examples and questions.

> *Answers*: **a** 3 **b** 2 Sentence **1** tells us the least.

Using 'ask', 'demand', 'inquire'

Discuss the three examples with the whole class, and encourage them to explain *why* one word is more appropriate than the other two, e.g. other phrases may give a clue about the attitude (Do you mind ...?) or the context may suggest a certain attitude (confrontation in a factory between the workforce and the management, as against the neutral setting of a travel agency).

> *Answers*: **1** demanding **2** ask **3** inquired

Understanding stress

- Read the first three sentences aloud yourself and discuss their meaning with the class. Then, have individuals read the three sentences aloud again.
- In pairs, students read aloud sentences 4–6, and discuss their meaning.
- To give more practice, select a sentence which has occurred earlier in the unit, write it on the board, and have students stress different words to change the meaning, for example:

> I'm looking for my wallet.
> Do you mind if I ask you a few questions?

Suggesting that things are easy to do

- Read the example aloud and have students repeat it to practise the correct stress and intonation.
- Do part 1 orally in class to give students practice in handling these longer sentences.
- Do part 2 in groups of 4, each student selecting one of the items (a–d) to explain to the other members of the group.

Reading and Listening/True or False

- Ask students to read through the true or false statements and to *predict* what they think the answers will be. Their own general knowledge will help them to make sensible guesses.
- Students then read the text silently, checking to see if their own predicted answers are true according to the text.

43

● Check the answers with the whole class, asking students to read aloud sections of the text which support their answers.

> *Answers:* **1** F **2** T **3** F **4** T **5** T

Explain

Students work in pairs. Student **A** takes items 1–3 and student **B** takes items 4–6. Give them a few minutes to work individually, looking back at the text. Then, with books closed, student **A** explains about cholesterol to student **B** who then explains about health to student **A**.

Language study: 2

What is the difference in meaning?

● Students discuss the pairs of sentences, working in groups of 3 or 4, and work out their meanings.

> *Answers:* **1** b **2** d **3** f

● Then, ask students to explain the meaning of the first sentences in each pair. Ask them to complete the sentences, using 'but', e.g. I never used to play squash but . . . (now I play it every weekend).

'be used to'

Read this through with the whole class. Ask individual students to read out sentences from the substitution table and then to make up their own examples.

Using 'be used to'

1–4 can be set as homework, together with the question 'What about you?'

> *Possible answers:* **1** They aren't used to driving on the left. **2** They aren't used to getting up early. **3** I'm not used to lifting heavy boxes. **4** They're not used to using Chinese chop sticks.

'consider' or 'regard'?

Give the students time to do the exercise individually, then check the answers with the whole class.

> *Answers:* **1** consider **2** regarded **3** regard **4** considered. Only 'regard' is used with 'as'. (*Or even things we regard as 'healthy', such as full-fat milk*)

Cause and effect

● Work through the sentences with the whole class, listing on the board the causes and effects, e.g.

Cause		*Effect*
high blood pressure	can lead to / can result in	many different problems
working too hard	is caused by / can be due to	a heart attack

● Then, in pairs, students look at the board and make sentences describing causes and effects. In addition, ask them to make up three more examples of their own.
● Look at this section in the Language summary at the end of the unit and go through the examples with the whole class.

Using the language of cause and effect

This exercise can be set as homework.
For extra practice in using the language of cause and effect, put a list of three or four topics on the board (selected according to your students' interests and experiences). In groups of 3 or 4, students choose one topic and discuss related causes and effects. Suggested topics:

unemployment	inflation	strikes
happiness	job promotion	ambition
examinations	urbanization	computers

STUDY SECTION

Writing skills

● Present this writing task by asking students what they know about 'town twinning'. (Is their own town twinned to another one? If so, what advantages does this have? Are there any exchange visits?)

● Read through the introduction with the class then look at the completed paragraph about 'ages and occupations'. Ask students what they think the original notes for this paragraph were like. Look at the notes for the other four paragraphs, and point out how important it is to combine and re-order information when writing out the notes.

Self-Check

Answers: **1** regarded   **2** used to complain   **3** considered   **4** was not used to   **5** asked   **6** the reason   **7** switch   **8** demanded   **9** been due to

The situation in this exercise could be developed into a role play activity in groups of 3 (Mr Evans, the shop assistant, the shop manager).

10   QUESTIONS OF CONSCIENCE

Overview of the unit

Lead-in: Cartoon-style story of a lay-about

Vocabulary (lazy, dependable, etc.)*

Reading: A nurse faces a difficult question
of responsibility
Comprehension work

Language study:
- doubt and certainty (he was
  obviously/he seemed to be . . .)*
- formal and informal styles:
  relative clauses (the hospital in which
  . . .)*
  passive (the patient was given)*
- word stress (hard-working; easy-going)

Find the dialogue: doctor and nurse in the
same situation as in the reading text
Comprehension work

STUDY SECTION
Writing: Complete a formal report with the
correct verb forms and write a report of a
visit
Self-Check: items marked * are included
here

Listening:
Full dialogue
between
doctor and nurse

Short answers
with 'I'm afraid'

Lead-in

Read the strip cartoon aloud to the class, and
ask: 'What do a lot of people say about this
man? Why do they say these things? Do you
think the man is very worried about what other
people say about him? (Why/Why not?) What is
your opinion of him?'

Vocabulary

After the class has matched *irresponsible* (c),
immoral (d), *unreliable* (b) and *a parasite* (a) with
their meanings, see if they can give you other
examples of each of these words. Explain that
you do not want definitions, but examples of
such behaviour. Give the class an example: 'A
friend was babysitting for some neighbours.
During the evening, her boyfriend phoned and
asked her to join him at a party. She went,
leaving the children alone in the house.' What
word describes her behaviour? (Irresponsible.)

Vocabulary study

- This is an extension of the *Vocabulary* exercise.
  Give the class time to study the sentences, noting
  down the 'good' and 'bad' adjectives.
- Check the answers with the whole class. Make
  sure the students can pronounce the words
  correctly.
- Ask students how far they agree with the division
  into 'good' and 'bad' qualities, e.g. 'Can
  someone be too honest/hardworking? Is it always
  a bad thing to be selfish?' If appropriate, the
  discussion can be broadened to include cultural
  differences in what are considered to be 'good'
  and 'bad' qualities. 'Are some of these qualities
  (e.g. generosity, modesty) considered to be more
  desirable in some cultures than others?'
- Students work in pairs for the next part of this
  section. (What kind of behaviour can be
  described as follows?)
- Give each pair three of the nine words to work
  on and ask them to write down their examples of
  behaviour.
- Then, the pairs read out some of their examples.
  The rest of the class guess which adjective applies
  to the example.

Reading

● Write a pre-question on the board to direct students' first reading of the text.

What is the problem facing the nurse?

● Emphasize again to the class that it is important to read through the whole text once without stopping when they come to words they do not understand.

● Check the answer to the pre-question after students have read the text (silently) once.

True, false or 'I don't know'?

● Students can do the exercise in pairs, then it can be checked with the whole class orally, getting students to read aloud the parts of the text which support their answers.

> *Answers:* **1** T **2** T **3** F **4** DK **5** F
> **6** DK

● At this stage, students can be encouraged to guess at the meaning of words they do not know e.g. *riddled, dosage, lethal, to draw up an injection*. This should give them confidence to make intelligent guesses using their own general knowledge and the context of the text.

Language study

What is the difference in meaning?

Discuss the examples and questions with the whole class. Then, ask students to say which of the following examples mean 'Perhaps I could be wrong.'

a) The train is obviously late.
b) The plane has apparently landed.
c) Apparently, this book is too difficult for you.
d) Obviously, this book is too difficult for you.

Tell the story

This exercise can be discussed in class and then set as homework. Remind the class of the difference in meaning between such sentences as 'I saw a light in the sky. It was moving.' and 'I saw a light in the sky. It seemed to be moving.' Ask the class which of these sentences they would use if they were not really sure the light

was moving. Notice the progressive infinitive constructions in the answers to 2 and 4 (*It/She seemed to be . . .ing*) and the perfect infinitive in 6 (*to have come a long way*).

Compound adjectives

All these examples illustrate the general rule that compound adjectives are generally stressed on the second element but with a strong secondary stress on the first element, e.g. ˌhard'working ˌwell'known
Students can use their dictionaries as they are working through the exercise if they wish (e.g. *flat-footed* will be found under the entries for *flat*).
Answers: 1 is flat-footed 2 is cool-headed 3 is kind-hearted 4 is thick-skinned 5 is underweight 6 overcharged (us)

Formal written language or informal spoken?

● Students work in pairs, discussing these sentences. Then, check their answers with the whole class. Even if your students never have to write formal reports, they should at least begin to recognize some of the different styles of language involved. Note that *whom* is rarely used in spoken English any more, except when the speaker deliberately wants to adopt a more formal style (as in official speeches, for example). Even those speakers who believe *whom* to be 'correct at all times' do not use it systematically!

Changing sentences to a more informal style:
● Remind students that they will probably have to change vocabulary as well as structure. Do sentence 1 with the whole class: 'The hospital I work in has a very good reputation.' Then, in pairs, students can do the rest of the exercise.
● After checking students' answers with the whole class, look at some of these very informal variants:

2 The documents you're talking about don't seem to be here.

3 You've got a hotel room right in the centre of London.

4 Sorry, we can't get the book you wanted.

5 My house needs a lot done to it.

6 The lorry the goods were in had a bad smash.

Using the passive in written English

This could be set as homework.

> *Answers:* **1** The patient's temperature was taken. **2** The patient was examined. **3** The injection was prepared. **4** The surgeon's instructions were followed exactly. **5** The matter was later discussed with the head nurse. **6** This matter will be reported to the head of the hospital. NB Only sentence **6** is likely to cause any problems. Sometimes, students attempt unwieldy constructions like 'The head of the hospital will be reported to about this matter.'

Dialogue

Find the dialogue

- Make sure the class understand the situation by reading aloud the introduction and asking 'Who are the two people talking? Where do you think they are talking? What do you think they are talking about?'
- Read the part on the left yourself, pausing after each speech to give students time to find the speech on the right which follows and read it out. Responses (b), (c) and (h) may cause problems because of their length. Be sure to give students time to get their tongues around these responses.
- Students then close their books. This time, as you read out the doctor's part, see if the class can remember (more or less) what the nurse said. Correct as little as possible, allowing approximate answers even if there are minor mistakes in them.

> *Answers:* **1** d **2** f **3** g **4** a **5** e **6** b **7** h **8** c

Explain the words

> *Answers:* **3** because he had a bad night and was in a lot of pain **6** increase his dosage of diamorphine to fifty milligrammes **7** the fact that I found his abdomen riddled with carcinoma **8** can't you accept responsibility for administering such an increase **f)** was in a lot of pain **h)** realize what it means when you say you found his abdomen riddled with carcinoma.

Listening and discussion

- Encourage students to predict what they think the doctor did or said.
- Play the cassette and see if students' predictions were correct. Ask students what they might have done if they were the nurse in this situation. This could lead on to a discussion of the degree of responsibility nurses have in different countries, or wider issues of responsibility and conscience in the medical profession.

Short answers

Students do this in pairs. Student **A** has his book open and reads the six questions, and student **B** replies (book closed). Then, the roles are reversed, and student **B** reads the questions but changes the order of them.

STUDY SECTION

Writing skills

- If the class did the Writing skills exercise in unit 9, explain that this exercise is continuing the theme of 'twinned towns', but this is a report of a visit by some British industrialists to their twinned town in Norway. Point out that the report is in formal language because this is a business report, not a diary of a social trip.

> *Answers:* **1** were met **2** were given **3** visited **4** was served **5** was attended **6** was held **7** were discussed **8** closed

- In exercise 2 (writing the report), encourage students to add extra details, e.g. they may want to comment on the speakers in the debate and the outcome, or talk about Lucy Lovell's poetry.

Self-Check

> *Answers:* **1** who was interviewed **2** obviously **3** She seemed to be **4** nervous **5** it was confirmed **6** in which Mr B. lived **7** apparently **8** it was not searched **9** to which Mr B. referred **10** hard-working

11 THERE'S A LOT MORE TO LISTENING THAN HEARING

Overview of the unit

Reading: Advertisement 'There's a lot more
   to listening than hearing'
Comprehension work

Words and their forms:
   efficient/efficiency, etc.*

Find the dialogue: Jerry talks to his boss, Mr
   Sherwin, who is not listening carefully
Comprehension work

Role play: Jerry
   talks to Mr
   Sherwin, who
   listens carefully

Listening: Two dia
   -logues between
   Jerry and Mr
   Sherwin: in one,
   Mr Sherwin
   listens carefully,
   and in the other,
   he doesn't
Comprehension
   work

Reading: Newspaper article 'Locked up 31
   years for knowing no English'
Complete the text with the missing words
Comprehension work

Role play: Hospital worker talks to doctor
   about Mr Tom

Language study: 1
- 'what' clauses (I didn't understand what
  you said)*
- 'which' clauses (You talk very quickly,
  which makes it difficult to understand
  you)*

Language study: 2
- word stress (Chinese, volunteer)
- gerund (listening is more difficult than
  hearing)*

STUDY SECTION
Writing: Completing a booking form and
   writing a letter of inquiry
Self-Check: items marked * are included
   here

Lead-in

A 'warm-up' phase to this unit can be provided by one of these activities:

- Students look at the title of the unit (*There's a lot more to listening than hearing*). Ask 'What do you think the title means? What other things, besides 'hearing', does 'listening' require? What makes a good listener? Why are some people 'bad' listeners? Which jobs need people who are good listeners?'
- Students look at and discuss the four pictures accompanying the text.
- Tell students you are going to find out if they are good listeners. First, tell them a short story, e.g. what you did at the weekend or a day when everything went wrong for you. Then, ask them to re-tell the story. Finally, discuss how well they listened and remembered – what information did they remember/forget/remember incorrectly?

Reading

Following the instructions, students read the text first for gist understanding and then answer the two questions. One procedure is to give them a time limit (2 or 3 minutes) to read the text silently, and then have them answer the questions, working in pairs.

True or false?

Students work in pairs on the exercise. Encourage them to answer the questions first without referring back to the text. Then, they can check their answers by referring back to it.

> *Answers:* **1** F **2** T **3** F **4** T

Focus on details

Students prepare this in pairs, then have the pairs report back to the class. The 'language of listing points' will be useful here, e.g.
Firstly/Secondly/Thirdly; The first/The next/The last; One/Another/A third ...

Explain the words

Students work in pairs, one with the book open at page 87 and the other with the book open at page 88 so that they can look at both the text and the exercise.

> *Answers:* **1** interpret, evaluate and respond to what we hear **2** the process of listening **3** listening

Vocabulary

- Without referring back to the text, students first read the definitions in question 1 and suggest which words are being defined, using their recollections of the text or their own knowledge of vocabulary. Then, in pairs, students refer back to the text and see if their suggestions are the words used in the text.
- Discuss with the whole class any differences between their suggestions and the answers from the text.

> *Answers:* **1 a** efficiency **b** evaluate **c** prejudge **d** prejudices **e** distort **f** ignore

Question 2 can be set as homework.

> *Answers:* **a** prejudices **b** distort **c** ignored **d** efficiency

Words and their forms

This can be given for homework, and students allowed to refer to reliable monolingual dictionaries, if they wish.

> *Answers:* **1** efficiency **2** interpretation **3** response **4** complexity **5** appearance **6** equality **7** distortion **8** ignorance **9** consideration **10** addition **11** attendance **12** division **13** expansion **14** convictions **15** amazement

Find the dialogue

- Allow time for students to read both 1–8 and a)–h) to themselves. Then, have one student read out the part of Jerry (1–8) and the rest of the class respond for Mr Sherwin (a–h).
- Students can then read the dialogue again, working in pairs.

> *Answers:* **1** d **2** g **3** a **4** c **5** h
> **6** b **7** f **8** e

Questions

Students work in groups of 3 or 4, discussing the questions. Encourage them to discuss the answers as fully as possible, especially questions 2 and 3.

Role play

- Read the instructions aloud to the class, and make sure that they understand that this time Mr Sherwin listens carefully.
- Students do the role play in pairs. Afterwards, they may enjoy hearing some of the pairs repeat their role plays for the whole class, especially if the outcome varies.

Listening

Students will be interested to compare the version on cassette with their own role plays as well as comparing it with the dialogue in the book.

> *Answers:* **1** Mr Sherwin finds out exactly what Jerry wants and agrees to give him some time off work. **2** He is a better listener in the second dialogue because he encourages Jerry to continue (Yes, go on Jerry. I'm listening) and asks questions to make sure he has understood (You mean nobody to look after your daughter, is that it?). **3** When answering this question, replay the cassette, pausing for students to complete what Mr Sherwin is saying, e.g. *In what way, Jerry? I'm not sure if ... You mean, nobody to ...*

Language study: 1

'What' clauses

Read the examples aloud to the class. Give them some more examples to work out, e.g. 'I've just explained something to you. Can you remember it? (Can you remember what I've just explained to you?)/I wrote something in my diary yesterday. I can't read it now. (I can't read what I wrote in my diary yesterday).'

Make one sentence

Do the first two sentences with the whole class, and then set the rest of the exercise as homework.

> *Answers:* **1** We must respond to what a person says. **2** We must evaluate what people say. **3** We often misunderstand what people say. **4** Listen carefully to what I am going to say. **5** I don't remember what I said yesterday. **6** Can you remember what you did yesterday? **7** Did you understand what I said? **8** Do you always understand what people say to you?

Using 'which' to stand for a previous sentence

In pairs, students study and discuss the examples. Check that they understand what 'which' refers to. Then ask them how they would write each sentence as two separate sentences (... *This* ...)

Make one sentence

This can be set as homework, after going over the first two sentences with the whole class.

> *Answers*: **1** Instead of listening, you talk all the time, which is annoying.   **2** You often interrupt instead of listening, which is not very polite.   **3** My boss never listens to what I say, which causes a lot of problems in communication.   **4** You never study or do your homework, which is why you will fail.   **5** Jack used to drink a lot, which is why his wife left him.   **6** She ran out of the room with tears in her eyes, which surprised everybody.

Using 'what' or 'which'

Stress that it is important *not* to think too much about whether to use 'what' or 'which' – if students have second thoughts about these sentences, they are more likely to be wrong. Students can do the exercise orally, working in pairs, before answers are checked with the whole class.

> *Answers*: **1** what   **2** which   **3** what
> **4** which   **5** which   **6** what

Reading

Ask students to read through the text quickly (and silently), ignoring the missing words. Then, have the class re-tell the story. They will probably be quite surprised at how much they have understood and remembered.

Vocabulary

In pairs, students fit in the missing words.

> *Answers*: **1** c **2** f **3** i **4** a **5** d **6** l
> **7** n **8** e **9** g **10** q **11** m **12** t
> **13** p **14** b **15** o **16** s **17** r
> **18** h **19** k **20** u **21** j

Ask and answer

- This can be done in groups of 4. First, students work in pairs, writing down questions to ask.

Then, in groups of 4, students ask and answer their questions.
- Finally, the groups of 4 think of three questions to ask the rest of the class (these can be some of their original questions, or new questions which they think of).

Role play

- Before doing the role play, students may find it helpful to revise the language of persuasion (if they have done unit 7, they should remember some of the language from that unit).
- Give students time to think about the roles, before they do the role play in pairs. After they have done the role play once, have them change partners, still taking the same roles, and do the role play again.

Where is the stress in these words?

The stress is on the last syllable in all the words. Answers 1 mountaineer 2 refugee 3 trainee 4 Japanese 5 Maltese 6 payee
Students can use their dictionaries as they are working through the exercise if they wish.

Language study: 2

Gerund

Read through the examples and explanation with the class. The term 'gerund' will probably be familiar to students at this level, and they can be referred to relevant sections in their grammar reference books.

Gerund and infinitive

Students do the exercise in pairs, then discuss examples 6 and 8 together with the whole class.

> *Answers*: **1** Doing ...   **2** Dealing...
> **3** Learning ...   **4** Prejudging...
> **5** Wandering ...   **6** To learn...
> **7** Learning ...   **8** To learn ...

For extra practice, ask students to make up their own sentences about 'learning English' or 'communicating in English'.

STUDY SECTION

Writing skills

- Introduce the exercise in class. Give students a few minutes to read through the text quickly, explaining that they need only obtain a general understanding of each course, in order to select one for themselves or a friend. Then, ask them, 'I'm not really interested in art, but I'd like to make my kitchen look better – which course should I go on?' (Elements of interior design.)
- Read the instructions about the letter. Explain to the class that they can ask about these things (expense, pet, books) in any order – they should think about how to paragraph their letter and the most logical order in which to ask for this information before they start writing the letter.

Self-Check

Answers: **1** Understanding **2** ignorant **3** To pass **4** what **5** attendance **6** complex **7** what **8** adding **9** which

12 WHAT'S WRONG WITH A LITTLE CRIME?

Overview of the unit

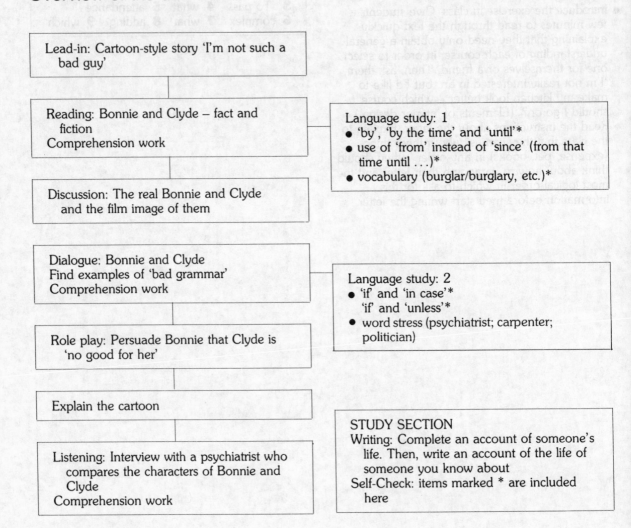

Lead-in: Cartoon-style story 'I'm not such a bad guy'

Reading: Bonnie and Clyde – fact and fiction
Comprehension work

Language study: 1
- 'by', 'by the time' and 'until'*
- use of 'from' instead of 'since' (from that time until . . .)*
- vocabulary (burglar/burglary, etc.)*

Discussion: The real Bonnie and Clyde and the film image of them

Dialogue: Bonnie and Clyde
Find examples of 'bad grammar'
Comprehension work

Language study: 2
- 'if' and 'in case'*
  'if' and 'unless'*
- word stress (psychiatrist; carpenter; politician)

Role play: Persuade Bonnie that Clyde is 'no good for her'

Explain the cartoon

STUDY SECTION
Writing: Complete an account of someone's life. Then, write an account of the life of someone you know about
Self-Check: items marked * are included here

Listening: Interview with a psychiatrist who compares the characters of Bonnie and Clyde
Comprehension work

Lead-in/Questions

- Read the text aloud, with expression. Then, ask students to think about the title of the unit and the character's comment that 'everybody does that kind of thing now and then, don't they?'. Do students agree that everybody commits a little crime occasionally? What examples can they think of? (tax fiddling, cheating with homework/exams, not paying bus/train fares, etc.)

- Students discuss the questions, working in pairs.
- Finally, in pairs, students read through the text again, underlining words they would stress if speaking. Then have them read out the text in their pairs.

Interpretation

Allow students to discuss the photograph in pairs for a few moments before opening the questions up for class discussion.

Reading

• Write on the board:

1909 __(1)__ born
1910 __(2)__ born
1930 __(3)__ met __(4)__
1932 Clyde and Jones __(5)__ a car and killed the owner of it.
1934 Easter Sunday: Bonnie and Clyde killed two __(6)__.
1934 May __(7)__

• Ask students if they recognize any of the names on the board (Bonnie and Clyde). Ask them what they know about Bonnie and Clyde – from films or what they have read. Then, ask them to read the text silently, filling in the main facts which are missing on the board.

> *Answers:* **1** Clyde **2** Bonnie
> **3/4** Bonnie/Clyde **5** stole **6** policemen
> **7** Bonnie and Clyde were killed in a police ambush

Questions

Students work in groups of 3 or 4, discussing the answers to the questions. Remind them to refer back to the text to support their views in question 1.

Discussion

• After discussing the photos of Bonnie, students may also be able to give examples of people who have been portrayed in films (e.g. Gandhi, Mozart) and give their opinions of the way this has been done.

• If appropriate, bring in some photographs (of you/your family/the town you are in) taken at different times and ask students to put them in

chronological order. Then ask them what clues they used to order the photographs, how they knew that some were taken years ago rather than recently and have them compare the differences in the photographs.

Language study: 1

What is the difference in meaning?

Go through the examples and comments with the class, then have students look back at the text to find examples of *by* and *until*, e.g. *by the time he was seventeen* (paragraph 2), *from then until* (paragraph 2) *by this time* (paragraph 3).

Using 'by' or 'until'

> *Answers:* **1** until **2** by **3** by **4** until
> **5** until **6** by **7** by **8** until

'From that time' or 'since that time'?

Have students work through the exercise orally in class, trying to work out when to use 'from that time' instead of 'since that time'. Sentences 1 and 2 provide a helpful contrast here – if the narrative is all in the past (sentence 2) we must use 'from that time'.

> *Answers:* **1** Since **2** From **3** from
> **4** Since **5** From

Teacher's reference: *A Communicative Grammar of English* **119, 154** (since).

Vocabulary study

• Read aloud the words 1–10 and have students repeat them to practise pronunciation. Pay particular attention to stress within polysyllabic words.
• Give students time to read the definitions (a–d) and match them. Check these answers before continuing the activity.

Answers: **a** 5 **b** 7 **c** 6 **d** 4

- In pairs, students work on the definitions of the remaining words, writing them down. To save time, give each pair two words to define.
- The pairs then read out their definitions to the rest of the class who have to guess which word is being defined. If students disagree about a definition, they could compare their definitions with those in a reliable monolingual dictionary.
- Go through the crimes orally with the whole class, getting students to follow the pattern 'A (criminal) is someone who is guilty of (crime)'.

Answers: **1** burglary **2** murder **3** theft
4 rape **5** arson **6** assassination
7 blackmail **8** hijacking
9 smuggling **10** kidnapping

Dialogue

- First, have students look at the picture and listen to the taped dialogue (without following the text).
- Tell them that they are not expected to understand everything after this first hearing, but ask them to listen and see if they can find the answers to these questions: 'What are Bonnie and Clyde talking about? What do they disagree about? How does Clyde defend his point of view?'
- Play the cassette at least twice and see if the students can answer these questions.
- Then have students follow the text in their books as you replay the cassette. This time, ask them to find examples of 'bad grammar'. (*I don't want to kill nobody/me neither/like when someone/yeah/I always says/they ain't.* Dropped endings such as *killin'* and *shootin'* and 'lazy' speech such as *keep 'em* and *don't wanna* may also be commented on.)

Discussion and interpretation

- Do questions 1 and 2 with the whole class, then have students discuss question 3 in pairs.
- Play the cassette again, students listening with books closed, so that they can see how much more they can understand now.

Role play

For variety, you could ask some of the pairs to do the role play given here between Bonnie and a friend. Other pairs could act out similar role plays on the theme of persuading someone not to carry on doing something, e.g. a teenager not to hang around a certain disco because you've heard that it has a bad reputation, a business colleague not to continue doing business with a certain company because you've heard that this company has a reputation for underhand dealings.

Explain the cartoon

Check that students remember the significance of the date (just after Easter when the two policemen had been murdered). Students can discuss the questions working in groups of 3 or 4, before exchanging views with the whole class. If appropriate, develop the discussion of cartoons – 'Are there any cartoons in the newspapers/magazines which you read? If so, what sort of cartoons are they? What do you think of them? Which cartoons do you like best? What sort of ideas are best expressed through cartoons? etc.

Listening

- For the first listening, students should aim for gist comprehension. Let them make notes as they listen, if they wish. After the first listening, have students re-tell what they can remember and write up notes on the board.
- Give time for students to read through the four statements, then discuss the answers with the class, seeing how many of the statements they can identify as 'true' or 'false' from the first listening to the cassette. If necessary, play the cassette again, pausing it appropriately to answer the questions.

Answers: **1** T **2** F **3** F **4** T

Listen again

- Have individual students read the questions aloud to the class. Then, play the cassette. Students discuss the answers, working in pairs.
- Play the cassette again before checking the answers with the whole class.

> *Answers:* **1** Bonnie had style, was more intelligent and warm-hearted. **2** She is not sure. The only evidence is the word of the farmer. **3** Because it smelt. **4** They built a fire to warm the rabbit. The policemen stopped, probably to investigate the fire. They probably did not know that Bonnie and Clyde were there. **5** Her warmer, almost motherly, character.

Language study: 2

What is the difference in meaning?

Teacher's reference: *A Communicative Grammar of English* **208–210** (if, in case, unless)

- In pairs, students study the examples and match them with their meanings.

> *Answers:* **1** d **2** b **3** c **4** a

- Have students complete these further examples, using *if* or *in case*: I'll go to the bank . . ./I won't go out today . . ./Would you like to borrow this book . . . ?

Using 'in case'

This can be set as homework.

> *Answers:* **1** I carry a revolver with me in case someone tries to rob me. **2** I'd better take my raincoat with me in case it rains. **3** I'd better give you my telephone number in case you need it. **4** Write down the numbers of your traveller's cheques in case you lose them. **5** Thomas has already built a huge shelter for himself and his family in case there is a nuclear war.

What is the difference in meaning?

Discuss the examples with the class. Then, have them complete the following using *if* or *unless*: I never phone people after 11 o'clock at night . . ./I don't buy clothes in the sales . . ./I can't get up early . . .

Using 'if' or 'unless'

This can be set as homework.

> *Answers:* **1** if **2** unless **3** unless **4** if **5** Unless **6** If **7** unless **8** if

Where is the stress in these words?

The stress is as follows: Group 1 and 2 have the stress on the third syllable from the end (psy'chiatrist; 'carpenter) and Group 3 has the stress on the penultimate syllable (poli'tician). Answers 1 psychologist 2 astrologist 3 novelist 4 physician 5 physicist 6 geologist

STUDY SECTION

Writing skills

Present this in class and draw students' attention to the language used to link chronological events, e.g. *eventually, when, by the age of*. Have students suggest other words/phrases which they could use in part 2 (Write an account of the life of somebody you know about), e.g. *before, after that, for the next few years*.

> *Answers:* **1** b **2** d **3** e **4** a **5** c

Self-Check

Introduce this in class by having students read it through quickly and identify what sort of note it is – 'Where do you think the note is?' (In some-one's house.) 'Who wrote it?' (The person who lives in the house.) 'Who is Maggie?' (A friend who is going to stay in the house while the owner is away.)

> *Answers:* **1** until **2** if **3** by **4** in case **5** unless **6** if **7** burglaries **8** since **9** if

13   THE UNCLE I HARDLY KNEW

Overview of the unit

Lead-in: Discussing a photograph of a room and speculating about who lives there

Reading: Bruno writes about his own life and the uncle he hardly knew
Comprehension work

Discussion and interpretation:
The lawyer's letter; the meeting with the lawyer; what would you do if you had just inherited a very large sum of money?

Complete the dialogue:
Mr Beale tells Bruno some good news

Intonation: Two meanings of 'What?'

Listening: Full dialogue between Mr Beale and Bruno

Find the two stories:
Good and bad news
Comprehension work

Language study: 1
● vocabulary (let down/out/on, etc.)*
● 'I feel like' and 'I feel as if'*
● vocabulary (sensation, impression, illusion, delusion)*
Language study: 2
● prepositions*

Language study: 2
● forbidding and saying things are not necessary/advisable (mustn't, don't have to/shouldn't, etc.)*
● word stress (photography; photographers; photographic)

STUDY SECTION
Writing: Matching four texts with their sources. Writing a hotel information sheet
Self-Check: items marked * are included here

Lead-in/Questions

● Before doing the Questions, ask students to suggest words to describe their impressions of this room. If necessary, start them thinking by writing these words on the board, and asking them which apply to this room:

comfortable   spacious   untidy   old-fashioned
airy   ornate

● Students discuss questions 1–3 in groups of 3 or 4. Then, exchange ideas in a whole class

discussion and see if their impressions are similar.
● Let students think about question 4 individually, making sketches and notes if they wish. Then in pairs, students tell each other about the rooms they have designed.
● A more general discussion can follow about different tastes and fashions in interior design or architecture. Students can discuss how preferences have changed over the last fifty years and predict what the trends may be in the future.

Reading/Explain and describe

- Read the first (3-line) paragraph to the class. Ask them to guess what might have changed the writer's life.
- Put on the board

father   uncle   18–22 years old
22–31 years old

Each student selects one of these four topics and reads the whole text, concentrating particularly on the chosen topic.
- Then, without looking at the text, the class answer the questions in Explain and describe. Together, the class should be able to answer all these questions.
- Finally, ask students to close their books and read the whole text aloud to them. Pause at appropriate points and ask students to continue with the next word or phrase, e.g.
I was born here in London but my parents ... (both came from Italy).
I went to Art School when I was eighteen but what I really wanted to study was ... (architecture).
I could hardly believe it. I felt like ... (jumping up and down for joy).

Discussion and interpretation

- Students can write out the letter in question 1 working in pairs. Remind students that lawyers often write in a fairly formal manner, and let them look back at the work on formal and informal styles in Unit 10, Language study: 2.
- Some students may like to act out the role play between the lawyer and Bruno after discussing question 2.
- Question 3 can be discussed in groups of 3 or 4, before opening it out as a whole class discussion.

Language study: 1

What is the difference in meaning?

- Students work in pairs discussing the statements and answering the questions. Check their answers orally with the whole class.
- Ask students to refer back to the text to see if the

idea in 1a) or 1b) was used (1b: I felt like jumping up and down for joy.)
- Students may find it helpful to look up *feel* in the *Longman Active Study Dictionary* and study the examples given there – *feel as if/as though* to have or give the sensation that; seem to be: My leg felt as though it was broken. *feel like* to have a wish for; want: Do you feel like a beer?/I don't feel like dancing now.

Using 'like ...ing' or 'as if I were ...ing'

- Give the students time to work through the exercise by themselves, then check it orally in class.

Answers: **1** like going **2** as if I were walking **3** as if I were going **4** like eating **5** like going **6** as if I were wearing **7** like wearing **8** as if I were talking

Vocabulary study

- Ask students to look at the four words and tell you where the main stress comes (second syllable). Then pronounce the words and have individual students repeat them.
- In pairs, students match the words with their definitions.

Answers: **a** illusion **b** delusion
c impression **d** sensation

The exercise can be set as homework.

Answers: **1** impression **2** delusion
3 sensation **4** illusion

Phrasal verbs

- Discuss the examples with the whole class. Ask students to suggest alternative (more formal) ways of saying the same thing, e.g. *disappointed her* (let her down), *gave* (let out), *reveal* (let on).
- Students can work through the exercise in pairs, then go over their suggestions with the whole class. Students can refer to good monolingual

dictionaries while doing this exercise as this will provide useful practice in dictionary reference skills.

Dialogue

Complete the dialogue

- Students work in pairs, first guessing the missing words and then checking with the list which is given.
- Then, in pairs, they practise reading the dialogue aloud, paying special attention to stress and intonation, e.g. in the 'What?' questions.

> *Answers:* **1** f **2** o **3** j **4** k **5** g **6** m
> **7** d **8** i **9** n **10** l **11** e **12** c
> **13** h **14** b **15** a

How would you say it?

- Play the recorded dialogue as far as:
  Beale: He's left everything to you. *Bruno:* What? This gives students a model to imitate. Students can compare this version with their own reading aloud of the dialogue.
- Students do the exercise in pairs, changing roles, so that each has an opportunity to practise the 'What?' in the responses.

> *Answers:* **1** pattern 1 **2** pattern 2
> **3** pattern 2 **4** pattern 1 **5** pattern 1
> **6** pattern 2

Listening

- Ask students to listen for all the extra information.

> *Answers:* **1** He introduced pizza to Australia and set up a chain of pizza restaurants. **2** He could not write. **3** He must use part of the money for his own further education.

Language study: 2

Which sentences mean the same thing?

Teacher's reference: *A Communicative Grammar of English* **341–344** (obligation, compulsion, prohibition).

- In groups of 3 or 4, students discuss the division of the sentences into two groups.
- Ask them, in their groups, to write down other examples about their school or their place of work using *don't have to* and *mustn't*.

> *Answers:* **1** b and f = prohibited; a, c, d and e = not necessary. NB *shouldn't* can indicate a weakened prohibition or negative advice. **2** a, d and e. **3** b, c and f. Students can refer back to Unit 3, where *should* and *ought to* are practised.

Using 'mustn't' or 'don't have to'

Read through the examples with the class. The exercise can be set for homework.

> *Answers:* **1** You don't have to tip the waiter. **2** You don't have to do this exercise. **3** You mustn't take photo-graphs. **4** You mustn't tell anybody my secret. **5** You mustn't park in front of that gate. **6** You don't have to explain this.

'Shouldn't' and 'don't have to'

Students can work out the exercise in pairs, then check answers with the whole class.

> *Answers:* **1, 4, 5,** = doesn't have to;
> **2, 3, 6** = shouldn't.

Changes in stress

Students can look up the words in their dictionaries to check stress patterns and pronunciation.
Main stress is as follows

1 illus'tration	'illustrator	'illustrative
2 'architecture	'architect	archi'tectural
3 'management	'manager	mana'gerial
4 'geography	'geographer	geo'graphical
5 'music	mu'sician	'musical

Review of prepositions

This can be set as homework.

> *Answers:* **1** as; by   **2** about; of   **3** at; from
> **4** at; in   **5** from/about; to   **6** to; to.

Writing

- Adapt the instructions to suit your class, e.g. if Friday, not Sunday, is the religious day of the week and if a mosque, not a church, is the place of worship.
- Students can write their four examples at home. Then, in the next lesson, they can work in groups of 3 or 4, reading out their examples to the rest of the group and making any necessary corrections together.

Find the two stories

- Read the two titles to the whole class, and ask students to predict what the stories might be.
- Then students work individually sorting out the sentences to make the two stories.
- In pairs, students compare their versions of the two stories and read them aloud to each other.
- Check answers with the whole class, and have two students read out the stories.

> *Answers:* Story 1: sentences 2, 3, 6, 8, 11, 12, 14, 16
> Story 2: sentences 1, 4, 5, 7, 9, 10, 13, 15

Explain and describe

- Allocate each student one of the five questions to think about. Give the class a few minutes thinking and planning time.
- Go through the five questions with the whole class, asking two or three students to give answers to each question. Encourage them to give full answers and allow them sufficient time before stopping them.

Explain the words

Students can work out the answers in pairs before checking them in class.

> *Answers:* **1** the lawyer; Barney Teller; the lawyer; Barney Teller   **2** the manager; Kenneth Davidson; coming to work with a punk hairstyle; Kenneth Davidson

STUDY SECTION

Writing skills

- Do part 1 (matching the four texts and their sources) in class.
- Ask students to underline language which gives 'rules' in these four texts, e.g. The only conditions are/No pets/cheques can only be accepted upon presentation of a banker's card/leaders of each group must wear the special badge.
- Discuss with the class what sort of information a hotel might want to give, e.g. meal-times, services it offers, its location and nearby amenities, fire notices.

> *Answers:* **a** nightclub   **b** farm guest house
> **c** hotel   **d** British Rail

Self-Check

> *Answers:* **1** as   **2** as if I were   **3** like
> **4** on   **5** to   **6** like   **7** it is forbidden to
> **8** don't have to   **9** mustn't   **10** don't
> have to   **11** on

If relevant for your class, this exercise could be used to introduce the theme of 'job interviews' and lead to a role play activity.

14 THE PRICE OF AN EDUCATION

Overview of the unit

Reading: A newspaper article about the conflict between the writer and her father over her decision to go to university
Comprehension work

Complete the dialogue: Eleanor's father encourages her to go to university
Comprehension work

Listen to the dialogue

Discussion and role play: Arguments for and against going to university

Reading: The end of the article
Sort out the jumbled text
Comprehension work

Language study: 1
- vocabulary (teacher, professor, etc.)*
- repeated actions in the past (he was always going/he kept going/he would go)*

Language study: 2
- he encouraged her to go/he discouraged her from going*
- making encouraging and discouraging remarks*
- stress and intonation (saying the same thing with two different meanings)
- gerund and infinitive*

STUDY SECTION
Writing: complete a confidential reference and write a reference for someone you know
Self-Check: items marked * are included here

Lead-in

One of these suggestions may be suitable as a 'warm-up' activity for your class:

i) Write on the board one or two phrases from the reading text, and ask students to discuss what they think the phrases mean and what they think of when they read them. For example
   the university of life
   The secretaries of today are the bosses' wives of tomorrow.
   generation gap
   What good is a university education to a girl?
ii) Have students read to themselves the first paragraph of the text. Then, discuss in groups of 3 or 4 what they think the story is going to be about and how it might continue.

Reading/Comprehension

- Use questions 1 and 2 in the *Comprehension* section as pre-questions to direct students' first reading of the text.
- Then go on to questions 3 and 4, having students read the text again and discuss the answers in pairs.
- The text can lead into a more general discussion of questions of equality in education and other areas, different ways of financing a university education (What happens in the students' own country? Is there a grant or a loan system?), ways of bridging the generation gap (Have the students any sympathy for the father's point of view? What do they think the writer should have done?).

Vocabulary

This could be set as homework.

> *Answers:* **1** understatement   **2** domestic
> servant   **3** generation gap   **4** feud
> **5** ordeal   **6** scold   **7** palatable
> **8** grudgingly   **9** texture
> **10** concession   **11** undermine
> **12** funeral

Discussion and interpretation

- Have students work in pairs, preparing a full
  answer to one of these questions. (Distribute the
  four questions fairly evenly among the class.)
- Then go over all the questions with the whole
  class, asking students to report back on the
  particular question they discussed.

Language study: 1

Vocabulary study

- Students work in pairs, discussing the differences
  between the pairs or groups of words and noting
  down their conclusions.
- Read aloud the definitions (a–l) to the whole
  class, getting students to match them with the
  correct words.

> *Answers:* **a** scholar   **b** student   **c** pupil
> **d** course   **e** examination   **f** scholarship
> **g** instruction   **h** training   **i** mark
> **j** grade   **k** degree   **l** diploma

- Then check the remaining words to make sure
  that all the students understand the differences.

What is the difference in meaning?

Teacher's reference: *A Communicative Grammar
of English* 120 (would)
- Discuss the three pairs of example sentences with
  the class and read aloud the explanation.

- Tell the students that sentences 1–8 re-tell parts
  of the text and so this should help them decide
  how to express the ideas. For example, sentence
  1 is probably 'kept saying' not 'was always
  saying' because the writer was not annoyed by
  this.

> *Suggested answers:* **1** kept saying
> **2** would help   **3** was always telling
> **4** was always insisting   **5** kept en-
> couraging   **6** would study   **7** would
> get   **8** was always complaining

What about you?

Give students sufficient thinking time then let
them exchange experiences, working in pairs or
groups of three.

Dialogue

True or false?/Find the missing words

Follow the procedure suggested in the book,
reading the dialogue silently, answering the
true/false questions and then finding the missing
words. Students can work in pairs on the
true/false questions and the missing words.

> *Answers:* True or false: **1** F   **2** F   **3** T
> **4** T.
> Missing words: **1** c   **2** f   **3** j   **4** e   **5** o
> **6** l   **7** m   **8** a   **9** d   **10** n   **11** b
> **12** h   **13** g   **14** k   **15** i

Listening

After listening to the dialogue and answering the
questions, students can work in pairs, creating a
dialogue between Jill Robinson and her father
which begins in the same way:
Jill: I was talking to one of my teachers today. He
thinks I'm university material ...
This will give you a chance to monitor how well
students can use the language of discouragement
(which is dealt with in *Language study: 2*).

Discussion and role play

- Divide the class in half and ask one half to note down arguments 'for' and the other half to note down arguments 'against' going to university.
- Then have a 'brain-storming' session with the whole class. This should give individual students sufficient ideas to give momentum to the role play.

Language study: 2

Reporting how someone encouraged/discouraged you

Have one student read aloud each prompt and another report it, using *He/She encouraged/discouraged me . . .*

> *Answers:* **1** He discouraged me from learning shorthand. **2** He encouraged me to take a course in computer studies. **3** He encouraged me to learn at least three foreign languages. **4** He discouraged me from studying domestic science. **5** He discouraged me from going to discos. **6** He discouraged me from starting smoking. **7** He discouraged me from getting involved with any boys now. **8** He encouraged me to keep studying and get a degree.

Encouraging or discouraging someone

Students work in pairs. Student **A** takes situations 1–4 and student **B** takes situations 5–8. Allow them sufficient time to think about what they are going to say. Then let them work through the exercise in pairs.

Saying the same thing with two different meanings

- Give students sufficient practice in recognizing the different ways of asking these five questions by saying them aloud yourself first.
- Then students work in pairs, saying the sentences aloud with the two different meanings.
- Finally, for each of the five sentences, students

suggest how the speaker might continue if he thought it was a foolish idea, e.g. What have you switched the television on for? You know there's nothing but rubbish on tonight.

Gerund or infinitive?

This could be set as homework.

> *Answers:* **1** to study **2** from doing **3** to learn **4** of learning **5** to go **6** speaking or understanding **7** of making **8** listening **9** at understanding and speaking **10** to going

Ask students to comment on the content of this exercise: 'Has your experience in learning English been anything like this? Do you think most students are afraid of making fools of themselves when speaking a foreign language?'

Reading

Find the story/Questions

Students work in pairs, sorting out the text and preparing the answers to the questions. Check the answers orally with the whole class.

> *Answers:* a g e b f d c
> **1** His generation had different attitudes to women.
> **2** She could not grieve for him and felt it would be hypocritical to attend his funeral.
> **3** She could have eventually forgiven him.

STUDY SECTION

Writing skills

Ask the class if they have ever written a reference for someone. If they wanted a reference for themselves, what sort of person would they ask to write it? If you write a reference for someone what sort of things do you write about? (What sort of things do you leave out?)

> *Answers*: Ex 1: **1** f **2** b **3** k **4** h **5** j
> **6** l **7** c **8** e **9** d **10** a **11** i **12** g
> Ex 2: **a** relationship with others **b** Work
> ability/potential **c** Personal qualities

Self-Check

> *Answers*: **1** from **2** secondary **3** would
> complain **4** from finishing **5** course
> **6** teachers **7** to **8** quarrelling **9** being
> **10** of leaving **11** Why don't

15 NIGHT AND DAY

Overview of the unit

Lead-in: Discussion and speculation about a picture of a city in the future

Reading: A talk by Dr Ella, one of the few people in the space colony who can remember what life on earth was like Comprehension work

Language study: 1
- using do/did and auxiliaries to give emphasis (I do miss them/I have learned a lot)*
- vocabulary – animals, their sounds and characteristics*

Discussion: Would you like to live on a space colony like this?

Complete the dialogue: In the space colony, a young child is asking Grandad about life on earth

Language study: 2
- describing the use and characteristics of tools, etc.*
- words and their forms (romance/romantic, etc.)*

Listen to the dialogue Comprehension work

Role play: A visitor from another planet asks specific questions about life here on earth

STUDY SECTION
Writing: Complete a text giving advice to British exporters to Japan and write a text giving advice to British exporters to your country
Self-Check: items marked * are included here

Lead-in

- Students can study the picture and discuss the questions in groups of 3 or 4. Encourage them also to compare this picture with other impressions of 'cities in the future' which they may have seen in films or read about in books.
- In the context of 'life in the future', ask students to consider the title of this unit (*Night and Day*). Will such a city as this have 'night' and 'day' or will there be constant artificial light?
- Continue the theme of night and day by asking: When does the difference between night and day become distorted? (Doing shift work/travelling through time zones/sitting up all night with someone who is ill.) How do you feel then? What is your 'best' time of day? Do you work best in the early morning or late at night? (Are you a lark or an owl?)

Reading

- Ask students to read the text for the main facts and to note them down. Then have students close their books (but refer to their notes, if they wish to) and ask them to re-tell the story. Make notes on the board as they are doing this. If there is any disagreement among the students, note this on the board as well and remind them to concentrate on clarifying these points during the second reading.
- Read the story aloud yourself the second time, and have individual students take the parts of Dr Ella and the students in the dialogue sections in the text.

Explain the words

This could be set as homework.

> *Answers:* **1** birds   **2** the student who raised his hand   **3** freedom (better than their present life)   **4** the few social undesirables who smoke and drink   **5** romantics (like the student)/experiments with freedom

Interpretation/Discussion

Students work in groups of 3 or 4, discussing these questions.

After students have discussed whether or not they would like to live in a space colony such as this, ask the groups to make a list of six questions which they would like to have answered to gain more information about life in the space colony. Groups can then exchange their questions, read the questions from other groups, and see if any of the questions are the same.

Language study: 1

What is the difference in meaning?

In pairs, students read these sentences aloud, discuss them and answer the questions. Then, go over the answers with the whole class, and ask individuals to read the sentences again.

> *Answers:* **a** 1b   **b** 2b   **c** 3b

Emphasizing what you are saying

Give students time to read through the exercise and decide where to put the emphasis. Then check the exercise orally, encouraging students to say each sentence naturally and fluently, rather than reading aloud word-by-word.

> *Answers:* **1** do enjoy   **2** does know **3** did get   **4** did hope   **5** does rain   **6** did get

Emphasis with auxiliaries

Read through this section with the whole class, having individual students read aloud the three examples.

Vocabulary study

Students can answer questions 1–3 working in pairs. Many good monolingual dictionaries have sections dealing with this area of vocabulary and may be useful for student reference (e.g. page

1298 *Longman Dictionary of Contemporary English*).

> *Answers:* **1** **a** 9 **b** 5 **c** 6 **d** 8
> **2** duck, cat, lion, horse, fox,
> **3** **a** lion **b** mouse **c** monkey **d** duck
> **e** cat **f** robin **g** dog, fox **h** horse

Question 4 can be used first to describe the animals pictured here. Then, in pairs, students can write down descriptions of another animal. The pairs read out their descriptions to the rest of the class who are allowed to ask up to five 'yes/no' questions in order to guess the animal. For example:

A: (reads out) This is a large bird with strong wings that eats small animals.
B: Does it live in this country?/Does it eat mice?/Is it an eagle?/Does it eat mice? etc.

Characteristics of different animals

- Discuss the two examples with the class (He ate like a horse – with a big appetite; He ate like a pig – greedily and made a mess).
- In pairs, students can then work on the matching exercise.

> *Answers:* **1** d **2** c **3** a **4** e **5** b

- Discuss the characteristics that certain animals have in different cultures, e.g. cats and dogs are regarded as pets/members of the family in Britain whereas in other cultures they may be regarded primarily as unclean animals. In English, it is common to say 'as wise as an owl' and 'as strong as an ox/a lion'.

Dialogue

Complete the dialogue

- Read out **A**'s part to the class, allowing time for students to think of possible responses after each speech. Students can then work in pairs, reading through the dialogue again and guessing what **B** says.
- Have some of the pairs read through the

dialogue, fitting in their own suggestions for what **B** says. The rest of the class compare these versions with their own.

Listening

- Play the dialogue at least twice for students to compare this version with their suggestions.
- Discuss the questions with the whole class.
- Then replay the cassette again, this time pausing after **A**'s speeches to see if students can remember what **B** says next.

Role play

- To prepare for the role play, take a simple item e.g. *a cup of coffee*. Build up an explanation of it with the class: 'What does it look like? What is it made of? Where can you buy it? What do you do with it? How much is it?' etc.
- Then students work in pairs, changing roles halfway through the activity. Give student **A** time to think about *football* and *drunkenness* and student **B** time to think about *catch a cold* and *night and day* before they start the role play.
- Each member of the pair can then think of two more things which they want to know about and ask their partner to explain them.

Language study: 2

Ways of explaining and describing

Read through the explanation with the class. Select an object from the dialogue (*wings, microscope*) and ask students to describe its characteristics and what it is used for.

What is it?

- One student reads aloud the explanation for each item (1–3) and the class identifies it.

> *Answers:* **1** knife **2** a personal cassette player, eg Sony Walkman **3** snake

• Give students practice in using the language patterns by asking them to write down descriptions of three objects seen in the classroom (or found in another specified place such as the kitchen, the garage). Students could work in groups of 3 or 4 on this. Afterwards, each group can read out its descriptions to the rest of the class, who try to guess what the objects are.

Explain and describe

In pairs, students select two or three of the items to describe, and write down their descriptions. Go round and check their work as they are doing this. Then, in groups of 4, the pairs exchange their written descriptions, read them and guess the objects.

Word forms

This could be set as homework.

> *Answers:* **1** scientists **2** scientific
> **3** exciting **4** excitement **5** freely
> **6** freedom **7** permission **8** happiness
> Check students' spelling of 3, 4, and 8

STUDY SECTION

Writing skills

• Introduce this activity in class, explaining that the text was written to help British visitors understand Japanese customs so that they would not give offence to their hosts.

• Prepare for exercise 2 by eliciting ideas from the students for one of the headings – if a British person is visiting your country on business, what is important for him or her to know about travelling in your country?

> *Answers:* **1** i **2** j **3** e **4** g **5** h **6** f
> **7** c **8** d **9** a **10** b

Self-Check

> *Answers:* **1** DOES have **2** DO go
> **3** barks **4** excited **5** is made
> **6** consists **7** like **8** was **9** can be
> **10** CAN be

LISTENING DIALOGUES

This section gives all the dialogues which are not in print in the Coursebook, including those which are variations of dialogues in the Coursebook.

Unit 2: Questions Of Honesty

Listen to what these two people would have done in Jennifer's situation.

Speaker A: Well, to be honest, I'm not sure what I would have done. I mean, it would have depended on various things.

Interviewer: On what, for instance?

Speaker A: Well, on ... hmm ... on how valuable the things the boys stole were. The text doesn't ... it doesn't say whether they had just stolen a tin of peas or something like that. So, I can't really say ... except well, ... I think I would have told the shopkeeper if they had stolen something really valuable. Otherwise, I suppose I would have just ... I don't know ... minded my own business, I suppose.

Speaker B: Well, I think it's quite clear what I should have done. The boys had broken the law. You can't allow that sort of thing to go on, can you? After all, it affects all of us. If you let boys or anybody else get away with theft, they'll just go on stealing! So, I think the woman should have told – what's his name? – the shopkeeper.

Interviewer: Mr Patel.

Speaker B: Patel. She should have told him and if necessary she should have held the boys while he got the police, or she should have gone for the police herself.

Interviewer: So you're saying that that's what you would have done?

Speaker B: Exactly. If I had been in that situation, that's exactly what I would have done. At least ... at least, that's what I ought to have done. That's what I hope I would have done!

Unit 3: Dangerous Illusions

1 Listen to the interview with Dennis.

Interviewer: Do you mind if I ask you why you've never got married?

Dennis: Uh ... well, that isn't easy to answer.

Interviewer: Is it that you've never met the right woman? Is that it?

Dennis: I don't know. Several times I *have* met a woman who seemed 'right', as you say. But for some reason it's never worked out.

Interviewer: No? Why not?

Dennis: Hmm. I'm not really sure.

Interviewer: Well, could you perhaps describe what happened with one of these women?

Dennis: Uh ... yes, there was Cynthia, for example.

Interviewer: And what kind of woman was she?

Dennis: Intelligent. Beautiful. She came from the right social background, as well. I felt I really loved her. But then something happened.

Interviewer: What?

Dennis: I found out that she was still seeing an old boyfriend of hers.

Interviewer: Was that so bad? I mean, why did you ... why did you feel that ...

Dennis: She had told me that her relationship was all over, which ... uh ... which was a lie.

Interviewer: Are you saying that it was because she had lied to you that you decided to break off the relationship?

Dennis: Yes, yes, exactly ... Obviously, when I found out that she had lied to me, I simply couldn't ... uh ... well, I simply couldn't trust her any more. And of course that meant that we couldn't possibly get married.

Interviewer: Uh huh. I see. At least, I think I do. But ... you said there were several women who seemed 'right'.

Dennis: Yes.

Interviewer: Well ... what happened the other times?

Dennis: Well, once I met someone who I think I loved very deeply but ... unfortunately, she didn't share my religious views.

Interviewer: Your religious views?

Dennis: Yes, I expect the woman I finally marry to agree with me on such ... such basic things as that.

Interviewer: I see.

Dennis: Does that sound old-fashioned?

Interviewer: Uh ... no. Not necessarily. What was her name, by the way?

Dennis: Sarah.

Interviewer: Do you think you'll ever meet someone who meets ... uh ... how shall I say it ... who meets all your ... requirements?

Dennis: I don't know. How can I? But I *do* feel it's important not to ... not to just drift into ... a relationship, simply because I might be lonely.

Interviewer: Are you lonely?

Dennis: Sometimes. Aren't we all? But I know that I can live alone, if necessary. And I think I would far prefer to do that ... to live alone ... rather than to marry somebody who isn't really ... uh ... well, really what I'm looking for ... what I really want.

2 Listen to the dialogue between Dennis and Cynthia.

Dennis: You've been seeing Steve again, haven't you?

Cynthia: What are you talking about?

Dennis: You know as well as I do. One of my friends saw you together in a restaurant yesterday evening.

Cynthia: Listen, Dennis. Look, I'm sorry. I was going to tell you. I really was.

Dennis: Well, why didn't you? Why did you lie to me?

Cynthia: I didn't lie! How can you say that?

Dennis: Yes, you did! You told me that your relationship with him was all over.

Cynthia: But it *is*, darling! It ended more than a year ago.

Dennis: Did it? Then why did you go out with him yesterday?

Cynthia: Because he phoned me and said he had some business to discuss with me. What's wrong with that?

Dennis: Nothing. But if that's true, why did you tell me you were going to have dinner with your mother yesterday evening?

Cynthia: Because ... because I thought you'd be terribly jealous if I told you I *was* going to see Steve. And you *are*.

Dennis: I'm *not*. I simply can't understand why you lied to me.

Cynthia: I've already told you. But you just won't believe me.

Dennis: That all you did was discuss business together? Of course I can't believe that!

Cynthia: Well, that's exactly what we did! And it isn't true that I lied to you about my mother. When I told you that, I intended to see her. But then Steve rang and said he needed my advice about something.

Dennis: About what?

Cynthia: A legal matter.

Dennis: A legal matter? Why should he ask your advice about a legal matter? You aren't a lawyer.

Cynthia: No, but you are! And that's what he wanted to talk to me about. You've been recommended to him. But before he contacted you, he just wanted to know if I thought you'd be willing to help him. I said I didn't know.

Dennis: Help your ex-boyfriend? Give him legal advice? I'm not going to do that.

Cynthia: That's what I thought you'd say. I knew it.

Unit 4: Who Needs Friends Like This?

Martin, Robert and Jean are being interviewed on the subject of friendship.

Interviewer: How important are friends to you, Martin?

Martin: I've never had a lot of friends. I've never regarded them as particularly important. Perhaps that's because I come from a big family. Two brothers and three sisters. And lots of cousins. And that's what's really important to me. My family. The different members of my family. If you really need help, you get it from your family, don't you? Well, at least that's what I've always found.

Interviewer: What about you, Jean?

Jean: To me friendship ... having friends, people I know I can really count on ... to me that's the most important thing in life. It's more important even than love. If you love someone, you can always fall out of love again, and that can lead to a lot of hurt feelings, bitterness, and so on. But a good friend is a friend for life.

Interviewer: And what exactly do you mean by a friend?

Jean: Well, I've already said, someone you know you can count on. I suppose what I really mean is ... let's see, how am I

going to put this ... it's someone who will help you if you need help, who'll listen to you when you talk about your problems ... someone you can trust.

Interviewer: What do *you* mean by a friend, Robert?

Robert: Someone who likes the same things that you do, who you can argue with and not lose your temper, even if you don't always agree about things. I mean someone who you don't have to talk to all the time but can be silent with, perhaps. That's important, too. You can just sit together and not say very much sometimes. Just relax. I don't like people who talk all the time.

Interviewer: Are you very good at keeping in touch with your friends if you don't see them regularly?

Robert: No, not always. I've lived in lots of places, and, to be honest, once I move away, I often do drift out of touch with my friends. And I'm not a very good letter writer, either. Never have been. But I know that if I saw those friends again, if I ever moved back to the same place, or for some other reason we got back into close contact again, I'm sure the friendship would be just as strong as it was before.

Jean: Several of *my* friends have moved away, got married, things like that. One of my friends has had a baby recently, and I'll admit I don't see her or hear from her as much as I used to ... She lives in another neighbourhood and when I phone her, she always seems busy. But that's an exception. I write a lot of letters to my friends and get a lot of letters from them. I have a friend I went to school with and ten years ago she emigrated to Canada, but she still writes to me every month, and I write to her just as often.

72

Unit 5: Success And Failure

Hugh is on the telephone. Listen to his conversation with Herr Kohler.

Secretary: I have a call for you on line one, Mr Gibbs. It's Manfred Kohler in Dusseldorf.

Hugh: Oh, yes. Put him through. Hello, Herr Kohler. How are you?

Kohler: Very well, thank you. And you?

Hugh: Just fine.

Kohler: Glad to hear it ... uh ... I'll come straight to the point, if you don't mind. I'm sure you know why I'm phoning.

Hugh: Yes, of course. About the ...

Kohler: Exactly. Are you in a position to give us a definite assurance that the goods will be delivered on time?

Hugh: Well, um ... you can count on us to do our very best, however ...

Kohler: Hmm. Excuse me, Mr Gibbs but I'm afraid that really isn't good enough ... I beg your pardon, I don't mean your best isn't good enough, but will you meet the deadline or won't you?

Hugh: I ... I was coming to that, Herr Kohler. I must be frank with you. We've run into a few problems.

Kohler: Problems? What kind of problems?

Hugh: Technical problems. Nothing very serious. There's no need to worry.

Kohler: I hope not, Mr Gibbs, for your sake as well as ours. I'm sure you're aware that there's a penalty in your contract with us for late delivery and we'll ...

Hugh: Yes, Herr Kohler, I'm perfectly aware of that. But do you need the whole order by the 24th?

Kohler: We would certainly prefer the whole order to be delivered by then, yes.

Hugh: Yes, but do you *need* the whole order then?

Kohler: What exactly are you suggesting?

Hugh: You can count on us to get half of the order to you by then.

Kohler: Hmm ... and how long before the other half is delivered?

Hugh: Another week at the most!

Kohler: Hmm ... you're sure that's all?

Hugh: Yes, absolutely! You can depend on us to get half the order to you by the 24th and the other half within a week.

Kohler: Hmm ... yes, that should be all right ... but there must be no further delays!

Hugh: There won't be! You can count on that.

Kohler: Very well, Mr Gibbs.

Hugh: Thank you! You've been very understanding.

Kohler: Goodbye, Mr Gibbs.

Hugh: Goodbye, Herr Kohler. And thank you again! Phew! Well ... that's at least one problem out of the way!

Unit 6: Voices From Nowhere

1 Mrs Long is talking to her neighbour.

Neighbour: Well, Mrs Long, how do you like it here?

Mrs Long: Oh, since we had the house redecorated, it's much nicer to live in. But there *are* still a *few* things that bother us.

Neighbour: Oh, what sort of things?

Mrs Long: Nothing to do with the house, really. It's just that our daughter, Jane, hasn't been ... uh ... well, she hasn't been sleeping well lately. I mean, she's had a few nightmares.

Neighbour: Oh, I'm sorry to hear that.

Mrs Long: Uh, excuse me, Mrs Woodside, but ... do you mind if I ask you something?

Neighbour: No, of course not. Go ahead.

Mrs Long: What ... what do you know about ... the people who lived here before?

Neighbour: Not very much. Nobody has stayed here very long since ... well, since ... you know ...

Mrs Long: Since? ... Since when?

Neighbour: Well, since those ... surely you must know about it?

Mrs Long: No, I don't know. What are you talking about?

Neighbour: Those terrible murders that happened here more than twenty years ago?

Mrs Long: Murders? What murders?

Neighbour: But I thought you knew! This house once belonged to a ... I really thought you knew ... to a man who's supposed to have murdered three or four women! Right here! In this house! Afterwards, he's supposed to have cut up their bodies ... right here ... in the kitchen.

Mrs Long: What? Are you serious?

Neighbour: Oh, dear. I hope I haven't said anything to ... well, to upset you.

Mrs Long: I can't believe it.

Neighbour: Neither could I. Not at first, at least. He seemed such a nice man.

Mrs Long: Who?

Neighbour: Taplow. Gordon Taplow. He didn't seem like the kind of man who could do such things, at all.

Mrs Long: You mean you knew him?

Neighbour: Yes, of course I did. Not very well, but I used to see him in the street occasionally ... We said hello to each other. He was a very quiet man. You wouldn't have thought he could have hurt a mouse. Once, I remember, he invited me in for a cup of tea.

Mrs Long: And what happened?

Neighbour: Nothing. I ... I never got round to it ... to coming in for a cup of tea. I was always too busy. I suppose it was a good thing, wasn't it?

Mrs Long: What?

Neighbour: That I never came in for a cup of tea.

2 A journalist has a strange story to tell.

I've never been a superstitious person ... never believed in ghosts or things like that. But, two years ago, something happened which changed my attitude. I still can't explain it ... somehow I don't think I ever will be able to.

I was living in Frankfurt ... in Germany ... where I was a financial journalist. A very good friend ... one of my closest friends ... we'd been at university together ... was coming over from England by car to see me. He was supposed to get there around six in the evening ... Saturday evening.

I was at home in my flat all that afternoon. At about three in the afternoon, the phone rang. But ... but when I answered it, there was nobody there ... on the other end, I mean. Nobody. The phone rang again just a few minutes later. Again, nobody was there ... I couldn't understand it. Just a few minutes later, there was a knock at the door. I was in the kitchen, making some coffee. I remember I was just pouring the boiling water through the filter when I heard the knock. I opened the door and there was my friend ... Roger, that was his name. Roger. He looked a bit ... strange ... pale ... and I said something like 'Roger, how did you get here so early?' He didn't answer ... he just smiled slightly ... he was a bit like that. He didn't say very much ... I mean, even when I'd known him before, he often came into my flat without saying very much. And ... well ... anyway, I said 'Come in' and went back to the kitchen to finish pouring the coffee. I spoke to him from the kitchen, but he didn't answer ... didn't say a word ... and I thought that was a bit ... strange ... even for Roger. So I looked round the door, into the next room, where I thought he was sitting ... and ... and he wasn't there. The door was still open. I thought for a moment that he'd gone down to the car to get his luggage ... and then I began to wonder where his girlfriend was. She was coming with him, you see, from England.

Well, then the phone rang again. This time there was somebody there. It was Roger's girlfriend, and she sounded ... hysterical ... At first I couldn't understand her. She was still in Belgium, several hundred kilometres away ... and she told me that she was in a hospital ... she and Roger had been in a car crash, and ... and Roger had just died ... on the operating table ... a few minutes before.

Unit 7: Sport And Violence

1 Three people are giving their opinions about boxing.

Speaker 1: When I look at a picture like this I feel ... hmm ... I feel ... I'm not really sure how I feel.

Interviewer: Disgusted perhaps? Horrified?

Speaker 1: No, no, I wouldn't say that.

Interviewer: Are you excited, perhaps?

Speaker 1: Excited? No, no, not at all. What's there to be excited about?

Interviewer: Well, a lot of people who go to boxing matches seem to be excited.

Speaker 1: Yes, I know. But I really can't understand why anybody should do that sort of thing, at all.

Interviewer: What? Go to a boxing match? Or box in one?

Speaker 1: No, the first. I ... I think ... well ... it's hard to understand why people should want to earn their living by fighting, but I think I can. I mean, it's the money, isn't it? No, I meant going to a thing like that and watching it. I ... I just can't understand it. That's all.

Speaker 2: Well, before ... I used to be disgusted by the idea of this sort of thing. Men fighting for money. Blood. All that sort of thing.

Interviewer: And now?

Speaker 2: Well, since I've started going to a few boxing matches with my boyfriend, I think I see something ... something else in it.

Interviewer: What?

Speaker 2: Well ... perhaps you'll be surprised when I say this ... but I think there's a real element of skill. Yes. Skill.

Interviewer: What kind of skill?

Speaker 2: Physical skill. Those men are really ... fit. And if you watch two good boxers ... boxers who know what they're doing ... you can see the skill. The way they ... they ... the way they watch each other and wait for an opening. That sort of thing. It's quite exciting, really. A bit like ... a chess game. Yes

Speaker 3: To me it's just disgusting. A brutal, disgusting spectacle. It ought to be banned. It sickens me ... the very thought of it sickens me.

2 An invitation to a volleyball match.

A: I've got two tickets for a volleyball match this evening. Why don't you come?

B: Uh ... no, thanks. I ... . I'm not very interested in volleyball.

A: Oh, why not? Have you ever seen it played?

B: No, I haven't, but I really don't th ...

A: That's what I thought. You don't know what you're missing.

B: Don't I? Why?

A: Because it's very fast, with lots of action.

B: Really? Who's playing?

A: Two of the best women's teams in the world, one from Finland and the other from Belgium.

B: Hmm. It sounds exciting.

A: Yes, it is! Very!

B: Hmm. Well, perhaps I'll come after all.

A: Good! Now ... uh ... could you ... uh ... could I have £5, please?

B: £5? What for?

A: Your ticket, of course. I bought two of them in advance, hoping I'd persuade you to come with me.

B: Oh ... uh ... You know, I've just remembered something.

A: What?

B: I've got to see some friends this evening.

A: Oh ... I see ... I mean ... you won't be coming, after all, then?

B: No, not unless ...

A: Unless what?

B: Perhaps you could let me have the ticket for a bit less? Let's say £3.

A: But you said you had to meet some friends!

B: Come on. I was only joking. Here's your £5. Of course I'll come.

Unit 10: Questions Of Conscience

Listen to the dialogue between the doctor and the nurse.

Doctor: Well, how's the patient this morning?

Nurse: He appears to have had a very restless night.

Doctor: Oh. Was he in very severe pain?

Nurse: Yes, I'm afraid he was, doctor.

Doctor: Hmm. In that case, I think we'd better increase his dosage of diamorphine.

Nurse: Yes, doctor. By how much?

Doctor: Let's see. How much is he on at the moment?

Nurse: Five milligrammes.

Doctor: Hmm. Increase it to fifty.

Nurse: Fifty? All at once?

Doctor: Yes, that's what I said, nurse.

Nurse: But that's an increase of forty-five milligrammes.

Doctor: I'm quite aware of that. However, when I operated on the patient yesterday, I found his abdomen was riddled with carcinoma. I'm sure you realize what that means.

Nurse: Yes, I do, doctor. But I still don't feel I can accept responsibility for administering such an increase.

Doctor: Can't you? What exactly do you suggest, then?

Nurse: That if you're convinced it's the right thing to do, you ought to administer the injection yourself.

Doctor: Hmm, I see what you mean. Very well, I will.

Unit 11: There's A Lot More To Listening Than Hearing

Here is an alternative dialogue between Jerry and Mr Sherwin. Listen.

Jerry: Uh ... excuse me, Mr Sherwin, but I was wondering if I could speak to you for a few minutes.

Sherwin: Well, I'm rather busy at the moment, Jerry. Is it urgent?

Jerry: Uh, yes, I ... I'm afraid it is. It's a personal matter.

Sherwin: Oh, well, then, we'd better discuss it now. Sit down.

Jerry: Thank you. Uh ... you see, it's about my wife. She ... uh ... well ... she

Sherwin: Yes, go on, Jerry. I'm listening.

Jerry: She's ill and has to go to hospital tomorrow. But we have a young baby, you know.

Sherwin: Yes, I know that, Jerry. You must be rather worried. Is it anything serious? Your wife's illness, I mean.

Jerry: The doctors say it's just a minor operation. But it has to be done as soon as possible. And ... well ... the problem is my daughter. The baby. That's the problem.

Sherwin: In what way, Jerry? I'm not quite sure if I understand.

Jerry: Well, as I said, my wife'll be in hospital for several days, so there's nobody to look after her.

Sherwin: You mean, nobody to look after your daughter, is that it?

Jerry: Yes, exactly. Both our parents live rather far away, and ... and that's why I'd like to have a few days off. From tomorrow.

Sherwin: I see. I think I understand now. You need a few days off to look after your daughter while your wife is in hospital.

Jerry: Yes, yes. That's it. I'm not explaining this very well.

Sherwin: No, no. On the contrary. I just want to be sure I understand completely. That's all.

Jerry: Will ... will that be all right?

Sherwin: Yes, I'm sure it will, Jerry. All I want to do now is make sure that there's someone to cover for you while you're away. Uh ... how long did you say you'll need?

Jerry: Just a few days. She ... my wife, I mean ... should be out of hospital by next Thursday, so I can be back on Friday.

Sherwin: Well, perhaps you'd better stay at home on Friday, as well. Just to give your wife a few extra days to rest after the operation.

Jerry: That's very kind of you, Mr Sherwin.

Sherwin: Don't mention it.

Unit 12: What's Wrong With A Little Crime?

A psychiatrist who has studied the legend of Bonnie and Clyde compares the characters of the two.

Shivel: Bonnie had something which Clyde completely lacked. Style. And she was also far more intelligent than he was. Without her, there never would have been a legend. He was just a rather stupid hoodlum who got into difficult situations almost by accident and then started shooting wildly. She was a much warmer, more generous person.

Interviewer: But she could be very ruthless, couldn't she? What about that policeman she shot in Grapevine, Texas? Didn't she laugh about it?

Shivel: Well, first of all, we don't know if that's what actually happened. A farmer says he saw her shoot the second policeman and then laugh. That's the only evidence we have that she actually did that. But even if the story is true, the whole incident illustrates this warmer, almost motherly, side to her character.

Interviewer: Motherly? How does the incident of shooting a policeman illustrate that she was motherly?

Shivel: Well ... uh ... just let me finish. You see, the day before the shooting, Bonnie and Clyde were driving about with a pet rabbit in the car. Bonnie's pet rabbit. Clyde started complaining because the rabbit stank. So they stopped and washed the rabbit in a stream. The rabbit almost died because of the shock of the very cold water. Bonnie got very worried, and wrapped the rabbit in a blanket and held it close to her as they drove on. Then, the next morning, when the rabbit still wasn't any better, she made Clyde stop and build a fire. She was sitting in front of that fire, trying to get the rabbit warm when the two policemen drove up and got out. Probably the policemen had no idea who was there. They just wanted to see who was burning a fire and why. A moment later, as we know, they were both dead. All because of that pet rabbit which Bonnie wanted to mother. And ... uh ... perhaps ... in a strange way, Clyde was something like a pet rabbit, too. She was attracted to him because he was weaker than she was and needed someone to mother him. It's strange, you know, but strong, intelligent women are often attracted to such men ... weaker than they are ... men who are like children, or pet rabbits.

Unit 13: The Uncle I Hardly Knew

Beale: Well, uh ... I'll come straight to the point. As you know, your uncle, Eduardo Gatto, died last December.

Bruno: Yes. I was very sorry to hear that, even though I hadn't heard from him for a long time.

Beale: Hmm. Did you know that he was a very rich man?

Bruno: Uh ... n ... no ... I didn't.

Beale: Yes. That's why I've come to see you. I ... I have some news for you.

Bruno: What?

Beale: He's left everything to you.

Bruno: What?!

Beale: Yes. The sum comes to more than two million Australian dollars.

Bruno: What?! I ... I can't believe it.

Beale: It's all true. In his will, Mr Gatto left clear instructions that I should come to London personally to see you.

Bruno: I ... I just can't get over it. I ... I feel it's just ... just too good to be true.

Beale: Oh, it's true all right. Believe me. However, there are certain restrictions about how you can use the money. Would you like me to go through them with you now?

Bruno: Yes, yes. Please do!

Beale: Well, first of all, you mustn't spend it all at once. The money will be paid to you gradually, over a period of ten years.

Bruno: Yes, yes ... I understand, but, before you go on, could you tell me how my uncle made all this money?

Beale: Pizza.

Bruno: Pardon?

Beale: Pizza. You know, the thing people eat, with cheese and ...

Bruno: Yes, yes, of course! But how could he make so much money with pizza?

Beale: Well, he introduced it into Australia just before it became very popular. And he set up a chain of pizza restaurants. They're very successful. He was a very intelligent, good businessman.

Bruno: It's strange that he never wrote to us. Never. I know he was very fond of me.

Beale: But he couldn't. That was his problem.

Bruno: Pardon? He couldn't what?

Beale: Write.

Bruno: He couldn't ..... Do you really mean he couldn't ...

Beale: Write. Even though he was very intelligent. And that brings me to the other restriction in his will. You must use part of the money for your own further education. Mr Gatto was a great believer in it. He always regretted he didn't get one himself.

Unit 15: Night And Day

A grandfather and his grandson are talking.

A: You lived on earth when you were young, didn't you, Grandad?

B: Uh ... yes, I did. But not for very long, so I can't remember very much about it.

A: Well, is there anything you *do* remember?

B: Hmm ... let's see ... uh ... yes, I remember seeing different kinds of animals on earth.

They have lots of animals on earth. Or at least, they used to.

A: Animals? What are animals?

B: Oh, things like dogs ... cats ... birds. Do you know what they are?

A: No, I don't. What ... what's a bird, for instance?

B: Well, it's a small animal with ... uh ... with wings.

A: Wings? What are wings?

B: Oh, they're something like ... like your arms ... but different ... without hands ... and ... and ... I'm sure you'll learn about them at school.

A: What are they used for?

B: For flying.

A: Really? Can dogs and c. .c ... cats do that, too?

B: No, they can't. Dogs and cats can't fly.

A: But why not?

B: Because ... because they haven't got wings, that's why!

A: Tell me something else, Grandad. Grandad? Are you listening?

B: Yes ... yes, I'm listening. What is it you want to know now?

A: Why haven't we got things like dogs and cats and birds here?

B: Uh ... well ... you see ... uh ... I'm not sure. Perhaps, because they carry germs around with them. I don't really know!

A: Germs? What are germs?

B: They're very small things. You can't see them.

A: But if you can't see them, how do you know they're there?

B: You ... you have to look through a microscope.

A: Microscope? What's a microscope?

B: It's uh ... it's something you ... you ... oh, why don't you ask your Mum or Dad ... or a teacher at school?

A: But I want to know now, Grandad! Why can't you explain it to me?

Longman Group UK Limited,
Longman House, Burnt Mill, Harlow,
Essex CM20 2JE, England
and Associated Companies throughout the world.

First published 1986
New Edition 1989

ISBN 0-582-03181-8

Set in Linotron 202 Souvenir

Produced by Longman Singapore Publishers (Pte) Ltd.
Printed in Singapore